A Practical Guide to Mentoring, Coaching and Peer-Networking

University of

Written for staff in schools and colleges, this book offers the challenge and support necessary for you to understand, analyse and adopt coaching, mentoring and peer-networking mechanisms as an essential part of the development of professional learning within your own organisation. Drawing on the national strategy for professional development, it emphasises the importance of learning with and from other colleagues, helping your organisation to become a professional learning community and supporting the drive to raise standards and attainment.

Organised into nine distinct but interrelated chapters, this is an invaluable source book of practical information for in-service training. It contains a range of stimulating activities which engage the reader and encourages reflection on:

- the nature and importance of professional development in schools and colleges;
- the potential benefits and difficulties associated with coaching, mentoring and peer-networking;
- factors essential to the successful establishment and management of coaching and mentoring programmes;
- team leadership and leadership coaching;
- the role of the coach, mentor and networker with respect to the creation of professional learning communities.

This book is for anyone with a responsibility for the mentoring of student teachers, the induction of new teachers and the professional development of experienced staff. It will also be useful for LEA and CPD advisers, as well as training providers.

Christopher Rhodes is Principal Lecturer in Education in the School of Education, University of Wolverhampton. He is Director of the Postgraduate and Professional Development Studies Programme.

Michael Stokes is Senior Lecturer in Post-Compulsory Education in the School of Education, University of Wolverhampton.

Geoff Hampton is Dean of the School of Education, University of Wolverhampton and Director of the Midlands Leadership Centre.

A Practical Guide to Mentoring, Coaching and Peer-Networking

Teacher professional development in schools and colleges

Christopher Rhodes,
Michael Stokes and Geoff Hampton

RoutledgeFalmer
Taylor & Francis Group

LONDON AND NEW YORK

First published 2004 by RoutledgeFalmer
11 New Fetter Lane, London EC4P 4EE

Simultaneously published in the USA and Canada
by RoutledgeFalmer
29 West 35th Street, New York, NY 10001

RoutledgeFalmer is an imprint of the Taylor & Francis Group

© 2004 Christopher Rhodes, Michael Stokes and Geoff Hampton

Typeset in Baskerville and Palatino
by Keystroke, Jacaranda Lodge, Wolverhampton
Printed and bound in Great Britain
by Bell & Bain Ltd, Glasgow

British Library Cataloguing in Publication Data
A catalogue record for this book is available from the British Library

Library of Congress Cataloging in Publication Data
A catalogue record for this book has been requested

ISBN 0–415–31778–9

Contents

Figures and tables

Figures

Tables

Activities

Preface

High-quality professional learning will have resonance with teachers at all stages of their careers, whether in schools or colleges, and forms the basis for improving learning experiences and attainment for learners in their charge. The national strategy for professional development in schools emphasises the importance of coaching, mentoring and peer-networking in assisting staff to experience relevant, focused and effective professional development. Learning with and from other colleagues, enhancing the impact of professional development, and embedding changed and improved practices are all essential elements in assisting organisations towards becoming professional learning communities and enhancing their drive to raise standards and attainment. This is also true within the post-compulsory sector of education. The rapidly growing demand for continuing professional development in further education coupled with the encouragement of staff to self-evaluate against the FENTO standards has resulted in the emergence of peer-networking, coaching and mentoring relationships. In addition, a growing demand for mentor training to facilitate the mentorship of new managers and those pursuing certificates of education within the further education sector, coupled with the emergence of executive coaching to assist in the development of effective leaders within schools, places this book as relevant to all staff in both schools and colleges.

The text and associated development activities contained in this book are intended to point colleagues towards the evolution of effective professional learning within the context of their own school or college. In order to achieve this aim, the book has been organised into nine distinct but interrelated chapters. Each chapter contains six activities to stimulate staff thinking and action and two extended activities, located at the end of each chapter, to further engage and challenge the reader with issues pertaining to the enhancement of professional learning, the impact of professional learning, and the use of coaching, mentoring and peer-networking mechanisms. Chapter 1 considers the nature and importance of professional development both within a school and a further education context. The chapter places coaching, mentoring and peer-networking as potentially very valuable mechanisms in raising the effectiveness of professional development, in ensuring the embedding of changed practice and in enhancing the impact of professional development within the classroom experience of learners. Chapter 2 continues to explore the benefits associated with coaching, mentoring and peer-networking relationships but also highlights some of the potential difficulties associated with the adoption of these mechanisms. Processes involved in the pursuance of coaching and mentoring are reviewed and the use of standards to act as precursors to the development of good practices is discussed. Chapter 3 offers the reader some insights into the establishment and management of coaching and mentoring programmes within the context of their own educational organisations, while Chapter 4 emphasises the unique nature of adult learners who will be the subject of support offered by coaching, mentoring and peer-networking mechanisms. Chapter 5 considers the key role of the team leader in securing collaboration, supporting staff development and in raising the performance of staff. Chapter 6 extends the theme of collaboration by exploring leadership coaching. The chapter draws upon two case studies and offers readers insights into the possible use of leadership coaching within their own organisations. Chapter 7 specifically considers the embedding of change and the role that coaching, mentoring and peer-networking mechanisms may play. Chapter 8 offers the reader the chance to reflect upon barriers to professional learning and its transfer to the educational experience of learners within their own organisational context. Finally, Chapter 9 reviews the role of the coach, mentor and networker within the creation of professional learning communities, and invites readers to consider whether the creation of such communities would assist in realising the full potential of professional learning within their own organisations.

In summary, it is intended that the book should offer the following benefits to the reader:

- knowledge and understanding with respect to increasing the effectiveness of professional development;
- challenge the reader to reflect upon the efficacy of coaching, mentoring and peer-networking as a means to change and improve practice;
- guidance on the development of these mechanisms within the educational context;
- assist in increasing the impact of professional development;
- prepare those in leadership positions to help others in embedding improved practices;
- encourage collaboration in the development of leadership qualities and skills;
- help staff to establish good standards and working practices in the use of these mechanisms so as to facilitate best impact;
- offer guidance on maximising benefits and in avoiding barriers to more effective professional development;
- take readers towards new and better strategies for their professional development.

This book does not present a step-by-step guide for all individuals in any educational context. Schools and colleges are different in their history and local context. It is certain that different organisations, teams and individuals within those organisations will have reached different stages in their journey to realising effective professional development and in the intensity of challenges they face. What this book does do, however, is to offer challenge and enable staff to reflect, analyse and consider developments which are applicable to their own organisation whether within the school or further education sector. Informed partly by theoretical texts, partly by research and partly by teacher experience, it is hoped that sufficient scope is left for individual reader creativity. The activities included may be addressed by individuals or by groups specifically within the context of their own professional circumstances. Coaching, mentoring and peer-networking continue to form a focus of professional development both nationally and internationally. Our own regional and local experience shows us that this focus may well be correctly placed. If this book contributes to the emergence of professional development within schools and colleagues which enables learners to achieve their best, then the time spent writing has been worthwhile. We wish all our colleagues in schools and colleges the best possible experience of professional development, and hope that they receive the support necessary to enable them to make the difference we know they want to make to the lives of learners.

Dr Christopher Rhodes, Dr Michael Stokes, Sir Geoff Hampton,
School of Education, University of Wolverhampton, December 2003

Acknowledgements

We are indebted to the staff of RoutledgeFalmer for their time and effort in supporting this book from start to completion. We would also like to record our thanks to the many colleagues in schools and colleges within the West Midlands who have provided the opportunity for us to undertake teaching and research activities which have informed the content of this book. We are also grateful to those colleagues in schools and colleges who have provided feedback concerning many of the activities we have included. In particular, we would like to thank participants in the University of Wolverhampton, School of Education, Postgraduate Certificate in Mentoring in Education programme, who have brought to bear their valuable experience. Finally, we would like to thank our families, in particular Sarah Rhodes, Annia Rhodes, Carol Stokes and Christine Hampton, for their support and encouragement as writing deadlines approached.

Chapter 1

Effective professional development

The internal and external environment

What is professional development?

In the United Kingdom (UK), a plethora of policy-driven initiatives, including the prescription of standards, enhanced self-management opportunities, organisational restructuring, professional development of staff and statutory interventions such as literacy developments, have underlain recent pressure and support by central government intended to raise the quality of teaching and learning in classrooms and, hence, standards in schools and colleges. Given that effective teachers are key determinants of successful learning, it is not surprising that some government initiatives have been directed at the management of teachers' performance and at supporting them in their professional development. Teachers are required to be competent in practice having mastered a body of knowledge. It is reasonable to assume that over time additional professional development inputs will be required to maintain the required professionalism. Professional development is regarded as an essential component in maintaining and advancing individual personal and professional abilities (see Friedman and Phillips, 2001).

For many teachers in the UK, professional development commences with initial teacher training, and in schools continues into the Newly Qualified Teacher (NQT) induction year. Teachers then engage with professional development activities, perhaps by necessity or perhaps by desire, throughout their career. Within the context of initial teacher training for schools, mentoring has become a familiar educational term in the UK. There is a rich literature concerning the role of the Higher Education Institution (HEI) tutor and related school-based mentor support during initial teacher training (see Hayes, 1999; Smith, 2000; Hopper, 2001). This literature shows that HEI tutors have important responsibilities with respect to the trainee teacher's placement school, the development and assessment of the trainee, and the development of school-based mentors who act as role models, support and encourage the trainee, offer feedback and assess the trainee against prescribed standards.

There is also a rich literature associated with the school-based mentoring activities of induction tutors during the NQT induction year (see DfEE, 1999; TTA, 1999, 2001; Bleach, 1999, 2000; Bubb, 2000, 2001; Hayes, 2000). NQT induction tutors in schools need to be fully aware of induction arrangements, possess the skill and knowledge to be able to make judgements against prescribed standards and to be capable of providing effective support for the NQT. However, it is not only at the early stages of a professional career in teaching that the support of a mentor may be required. For example, experienced staff in either schools or colleges may need the support of a mentor at the start of a new post. In this case, the mentoring relationship is likely to take the form of a sensitively managed partnership designed to enable new staff to quickly adopt the working practices of the new institution and bring their own skills to bear as soon as possible (see Fabian and Simpson, 2002).

Although professional development during initial teacher training, during the NQT induction period and for staff commencing in new posts is of great importance, this text is concerned primarily with the professional development of teachers in schools and colleges who are established in their present posts, are experienced, and either seek to engage in or are required to engage in professional learning. Professional development in this context has often been referred to as continuing professional development (CPD). It is well established that the continuing professional development of teachers is regarded as essential in creating effective educational organisations and in raising the standards of learner achievement (see Kydd *et al.*, 1997; O'Brien and MacBeath, 1999; Moon, 2000). For example, professional development has been associated with improving classroom performance, engaging with opportunities created by change initiatives, preparing teachers for specialist roles within the organisation, preparing teachers for roles in management and leadership, and enabling the sharing of good practices through networking arrangements. Professional development has been defined in *Learning and Teaching: A Strategy for Professional Development* (DfES, 2001a) as: 'any activity that increases the skills, knowledge or understanding of teachers, and their effectiveness in schools.'

Activity 1.1

How are your personal and professional needs identified?

The following diagram depicts a possible professional development cycle:

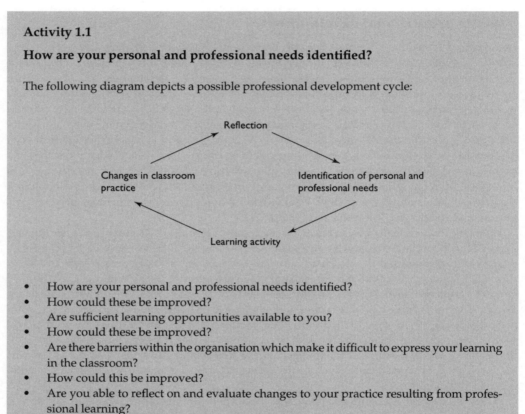

- How are your personal and professional needs identified?
- How could these be improved?
- Are sufficient learning opportunities available to you?
- How could these be improved?
- Are there barriers within the organisation which make it difficult to express your learning in the classroom?
- How could this be improved?
- Are you able to reflect on and evaluate changes to your practice resulting from professional learning?
- How could this be improved?

How do teachers acquire professional knowledge?

Gains in professional knowledge may be generated in a number of different ways. For example, teachers may find that they acquire professional knowledge by attending courses, or they may generate knowledge through their own experience of teaching. Alternatively, they may acquire knowledge through collaboration and discourse with other teachers either from the same or from other organisations.

With respect to knowledge acquisition, Sugrue (2002), drawing on the work of Cochran-Smith and Lytle (1999), suggests that three broad conceptualisations as points on a continuum are identifiable in the teacher continuing professional development literature:

1   *Knowledge for practice*

Teachers engage with instruction and bring back 'best practices' generated by researchers which can be applied within their own practice. This equates broadly to 'course' attendance on the part of teachers.

2   *Knowledge in practice*

Teachers themselves generate 'best practices' and modify their own practices accordingly. This implies reflective practice on the part of teachers either individually or as part of a group and suggests that the parent organisation is able to sustain at least some characteristics of a learning community.

3   *Knowledge of practice*

Teachers are active in their own learning, and are engaged in enquiry and the construction of new insights through collaborative learning in groups, communities and networks.

Activity 1.2

Gaining professional knowledge

How does your organisation enable staff to gain:

- Knowledge for practice?
- Knowledge in practice?
- Knowledge of practice?
- Which kind of knowledge acquisition is best supported?
- Which kind of knowledge acquisition is least well supported?
- How could this be improved?

An organisational climate for professional development

The establishment of a climate in which open networking between colleagues enables mutual support and reflection to take place has been shown to be an important element in the effective management of school professional development cultures (see Law and Glover, 1996). However, not all schools benefit from the presence of such a climate (see Law, 1999). In educational organisations, leadership and management teams should consider whether staff collaboration is facilitated or hindered by the professional development culture they have created. For example, Williams *et al.* (2001) point out that support and development accorded to newly qualified teachers is of a much higher order in schools where the culture is one of collaboration when compared to schools with cultures denoted by individualism.

Organisational leadership and management exercises significant influence on teacher professional development. For example, a study by Bredeson and Johansson (2000) identified four areas where school principals have the opportunity to effect a substantial impact on teacher learning:

1   The principal as an instructional leader and learner;
2   The creation of a learning environment;
3   Direct involvement in the design, delivery and content of professional development;
4   The assessment of professional development outcomes.

In order that school leadership and management teams may create cultures which link teacher professional development more firmly to the achievement of objectives, a system of performance management came into statutory force in September 2000 for schools in England. The performance management framework (see DfEE, 2000a, b) leads teachers to expect a focus upon the improvement of their knowledge and skills, and also offers financial reward for those who are deemed to be performing well. Performance management may be viewed as an important element in raising professional standards or as an element of governmental intervention to exact greater efficiency, effectiveness and accountability (see Down *et al.*, 1999; Gleeson and Husbands, 2001).

In essence, performance management is meant to identify teacher strengths and weaknesses with respect to addressing performance targets set so that development needs are identified and recognised. However, doubts have been raised concerning the management of teacher performance in this way, since as teaching practices take time to develop, requiring reflection on experience rather than being amenable to rapid change through the direct intervention of performance management mechanisms (see Silcock, 2002). Feedback on performance management from schools in England has revealed the following:

- The emotional climate of an organisation is important in effecting improvement. Highly motivated staff are likely to drive up performance.
- The approach of current performance management arrangements does not connect with the learning of some teachers and simply brings about 'performing for the management'.
- There is a linkage between staff relationships based upon mutual respect, collaboration and consultation and which involve a 'feel-good' factor, and the high levels of intrinsic motivation leading to the use of initiative and a desire on the part of staff to achieve high-quality work.
- Where performance management is a 'bolt-on' activity, it has little impact upon learner progress, the performance of staff or the overall achievement of the organisation.

Activity 1.3

Emotional climate and performance management

- Rate the emotional climate of your organisation on a scale from 1 (low) to 10 (high). What factors tend to drive this up? What factors tend to drive this down?
- Rate the relationship of your access to professional development with your performance management or appraisal arrangements on a scale of 1 (low) to 10 (high). What factors tend to drive this up? What factors tend to drive this down?
- Rate the 'feel-good' factor of staff relationships within your organisation on a scale from 1 (low) to 10 (high). What factors tend to drive this up? What factors tend to drive this down?
- Rate the impact of performance management or appraisal arrangements on learner or staff performance within your organisation on a scale from 1 (low) to 10 (high). What factors tend to drive this up? What factors tend to drive this down?

Leaders, whether in schools or colleges, can influence the culture and purpose of their organisations and, as such, they are able to create an environment which can influence job-related attitudes. Evans (2001) suggests that leadership can shape work contexts that either match or are at odds with what individuals want in relation to equity and justice, organisational efficiency, interpersonal relations, collegiality and self-conception and self-image. School and college leaders can make significant interventions to enhance the working lives of teachers. They can influence the emotional climate of their organisations and, in so doing, motivate staff and impact positively upon teachers' working lives. In view of the extensive methodology available to access cultural information within organisations (see e.g. Locatelli and West, 1996; Higgins-D'Alessandro and Sadh, 1997; Cartwright *et al.*, 1999), school and college leadership training should perhaps include stronger emphasis on cultural change methodology aimed at improving teacher professional experience, satisfaction and increasing the likelihood of retention.

Professional development and teacher retention

The seeds of non-retention within the profession are sown at an early stage. In a study of students who had been successfully recruited to primary initial teacher education courses, Thornton *et al.* (2002) showed that students held deep concerns about their subsequent pay, workload, media image, status, hours, paperwork and stress levels. Visions of low status, demotivation and worsening retention of serving teachers is likely to present a discouraging image for those who are considering entering the profession. A survey undertaken for the General Teaching Council in England (GTC, 2002) showed that falling morale is impacting on intentions to stay within the profession, with one in three teachers not expecting still to be teaching in five years' time.

The linkage between professional development and teacher retention has received much recent attention. Dean (2001) suggests that premature loss of experienced teachers may be curtailed or prevented through professional development activities such as sabbaticals which would allow for personal refreshment. An Ofsted (2003) evaluation of the quality and effectiveness of early professional development undertaken by teachers suggested that in about half of the schools in the survey (n = 61) teachers felt that development activities had strengthened their commitment to a career in teaching. Rowe and Sykes (1989) have found the potential for strong positive effects of professional development on teachers' professional self-perceptions, energy, enthusiasm and satisfaction. Beatty (2000) has shown that self-directed professional learning, personal and shared reflection, and authentic collaboration in a supportive study group environment can create changes in teachers' perceptions of themselves and their work and catalyse professional growth. A report by Day *et al.* (2002) has suggested that provision of opportunities for teachers to reflect on their teaching and engage in dialogue about it with other teachers can help to build motivation and commitment. Given that teacher collaboration and mutual support offer the potential to raise teacher confidence and facilitate teacher professional learning (see Rhodes and Beneicke, 2002), school and college leadership teams need to consider how productive collaboration can be engendered within the context of their own organisations, how they might remove obstacles to sharing and how they may offer support as well as challenge. Emphasising the importance of school leadership with respect to the outcomes experienced by teachers engaging in professional development, Earley *et al.* (2002) have recommended that a key component of leadership programmes should include managing professional development for others as well as inclusion of theoretical frameworks which underpin professional learning.

Activity 1.4

Professional development and teacher retention

A recent survey of teacher job satisfaction undertaken within an English LEA (Rhodes C.P., Nevill, A. and Allan, J. L. in press) yielded 368 questionnaires from teachers about facets of their professional experience which they found to be deeply satisfying or deeply dissatisfying. Here are some of the results:

Facet	% of sample	% Deeply satisfying	% Deeply dissatisfying
Workload	58	4 (n = 8)	96 (n = 206)
Balance between work and personal life	51	17 (n = 32)	83 (n = 155)
Friendliness of other staff	44	97 (n = 156)	3 (n = 5)
Impact of performance management	15	2 (n = 1)	98 (n = 55)
Professional development is offered which is relevant to my own needs	6	48 (n = 11)	52 (n = 12)

continued

- Why might teachers rank 'professional development which is relevant to my own needs' so lowly?
- What advice would you give to the LEA?
- What advice would you give to the schools?
- What advice would you give to the teachers?
- Would you expect teachers to rank 'professional development which is relevant to my own needs' so lowly in your own organisation?
- What steps would you take to ensure that professional development could enhance retention within your own organisation?

A national strategy for professional development?

The school context

The national strategy for continuing professional development in the UK (DfES, 2001a) espouses a desire to give teachers greatly increased opportunities for relevant, focused, effective professional development, and to place professional development at the heart of school improvement. A code of practice for providers of professional development (DfES, 2001b) emphasises the need to maximise the impact of professional development by closely identifying development needs, linking the benefits to meeting the needs of individual teachers and also linking benefits of training to improvements to be experienced by pupils in the classroom.

The measurement of impact is problematical but draws those providing and those experiencing professional development to consider organisational translation of professional development into improved classroom learning and learner performance (see Rhodes and Houghton-Hill, 2000). Impact should not, however, be concerned solely with quantifiable data of learning gains for learners but also take into account teachers' own personal, academic and professional needs. Given that teachers will have unique patterns of individual professional learning, Burchell *et al.* (2002) argue that there are different ways to demonstrate impact which include hard tangible outcomes, and also affective and motivational outcomes rooted in personal and professional values. Davies and Preston (2002) also emphasise the personal as well as the professional impact of professional development. Barriers to the transfer of teacher learning to pupil learning have been shown to exist in some schools, and school leaders and managers themselves are implicated in the creation of such barriers (Rhodes and Houghton-Hill, 2000). School leaders and managers need to examine the systems they have created, which may impede the expression of teacher learning in classrooms. The transfer of learning to new contexts has long been the topic of debate in the research community (see Alexander and Murphy, 1999). A helpful distinction between near and far transfer has been made by Simons (1999). Near transfer is characterised by a close relationship between the learning situation and the application of learning, whereas in far transfer the distance between learning and its application is much greater. Pursuance of near transfer to impact upon immediate difficulties would ideally be coupled with consideration of far transfer so as to allow continued professional growth. It is therefore desirable that any feedback offered to teachers in this context goes beyond the level of mechanistic direction and also offers the opportunity to reflect deeply on their practice. The expression of explicit learning goals for teachers is not enough. Leaders and managers need to offer support within the work environment which ensures that teachers have the opportunity to use learned knowledge and skills in conjunction with feedback which encourages reflection. West-Burnham and O'Sullivan (1998) point out that both coaching and reflection are required in order to produce a consolidated and internalised learning experience, and Thompson (2001) has suggested that coaching without reflection will not enable learning to take place.

As part of the national strategy for professional development and as a guide to identifying possible areas for professional development, The Teachers' Standards Framework (DfES, 2001c) presents ten dimensions of teaching and leadership, and relates these to the role expectations of teachers from gaining qualified teacher status to becoming headteacher.

The Teachers' Standards Framework also emphasises professional development activities thought to have the most impact on classroom practice.

1   Opportunities to learn from and with other teachers in their own or other schools by:

   •   observing colleagues teaching and discussing this;
   •   working together on real school improvement problems, drawing on best practice in developing solutions;
   •   taking part in coaching or mentoring.

2   High-quality focused training on specific skill areas underpinned by excellent teaching materials and direct support to apply teachers' learning back into the classroom.

3   Teachers are receptive to change, particularly because they believe it will help their pupils' learning and where development involves:

   •   a focus upon specific teaching and learning problems;
   •   opportunities for teachers to reflect on what they know and do already;
   •   opportunities for teachers to understand the rationale behind new ideas and approaches; to see theory demonstrated in practice, and to be exposed to new expertise;
   •   sustained opportunities to experiment with new ideas and approaches, so that teachers can work out their implications for their own subject, pupils, school and community;
   •   opportunities for teachers to put their own interpretation of new strategies and ideas to work, building on their existing knowledge and skills;
   •   coaching and feedback on their changing practice on a sustained basis over a period of weeks and months. This is a particularly important element and can be decisive in determining whether changes in practice survive.

4   Teachers are supported by their headteachers or heads of departments, and by participation in wider teacher networks.

Activity 1.5

An audit of professional development in relation to the Teachers' Standards Framework

   •   How many of the above list of professional development activities from the Teachers' Standards Framework can you identify within your own professional context?
   •   Which are undertaken well?
   •   Which require further development to enhance impact on classroom practice?

The further education context

Colleges in the further education sector too have been in receipt of government initiatives concerned with staff professional development. Most staff development has been directly linked to government initiatives and the priorities set by the Manpower Services Commission (MSC), the Further Education Funding Council (FEFC), the training and enterprise Councils (TECs) and the Learning and Skills Council (LSC) since the mid-1980s. Until recently, many of these initiatives were linked to the quality and diversity of vocational programmes that were in turn linked to youth or adult training. Such initiatives have had a mixed reception from colleges. Since 1993, unlike schools, colleges have been required to manage local further education without the reins of a Local Education Authority (LEA). Operating within the funding methodology of FEFC has enabled colleges to develop their own slant on new initiatives by acting within the general spirit of such developments. Given that funding has been related to student numbers and learner success, colleges have sought growth in student numbers to maintain their income. Competition for student growth has been a signal for many colleges to 'go it alone', seeing other colleges as rivals. In such an environment it is not uncommon for staff development to become deprioritised.

Notwithstanding this, the FEFC began to allocate some funds specifically to support professional development in the delivery of the government priorities. Funding strongly encouraged staff development planning to be taken seriously within a framework prescribed by the FEFC. This framework linked staff development to the priorities set out in the FEFC strategic plan. For example, the priorities for 1999/00 (FEFC, 1999) were fourfold:

1   first and foremost targeting intervention in colleges causing concern, notably those demonstrating poor performance against key indicators;
2   post-inspection support for other colleges, as appropriate;
3   training for existing and potential college principals, and continuing professional development for lecturers;
4   dissemination of good practice.

Each priority was associated with levels of funding to ensure that colleges produced plans to meet these priorities. At the end of 1999 the Department for Education and Skills (DfES) introduced Curriculum 2000, a plan to change full-time programmes for 16- to 18-year-olds in all post-16 schools and colleges. Such a far reaching cross-sector initiative demanded new approaches to teaching and learning, and increased knowledge and skills in further education staff. With it came a standards fund for the 2000/01 academic year (FEFC, 2000) containing changes to its priorities to include staff development for Curriculum 2000. It was made explicit that funding would be made available to support the development of methods to identify staff who demonstrate excellence in their work and have the ability to mentor other staff.

The purpose of such mentoring would be to:

•   support new staff;
•   assist part-time staff in improving their performance;
•   support under-performing staff;
•   develop staff for promotion.

This was recognition that staff development for improved performance could be enhanced by receiving the support of others. The fund also had a category for the 'Dissemination of Good Practice' which, at this time, was not seen as being supported by mentors.

New legislation (Statutory Instrument 2001, No. 1209) determined that all new lecturers in further education from September 2001 should be trained and have a further education teachers' qualification, and that those already in post should be encouraged to gain a teaching qualification. The qualifications were to be based on the 'standards' provided by the Further Education National Training Organisation (FENTO). The new Labour government provided a funding stimulus to 'kick-start' this qualification drive through the Teachers' Pay Initiative (DfEE, 2001a) which supported colleges, if they so wished, to provide financial incentives for staff to become qualified. This initiative also provided financial incentives for staff to engage in continuing professional development in order to improve the standard of their teaching and their student's learning.

The FENTO teaching standards have been developed in consultation with colleges and after several iterations were agreed in 2001. They were to be used for designing accredited awards for further education (FE) teachers; to inform professional development; and to assist in appraisal and identification of training needs. The standards consist of three main elements: professional knowledge and understanding; skills and attributes; and key areas of teaching. Informing the Standards (FENTO, 2001) were a set of values that included reflective practice and scholarship: 'The ability of teachers to reflect upon their practice and to apply appropriate methods, therefore, is a crucial one which any set of standards would seek to promote.'

The Standards have been developed to cover all the major areas of activity:

- assessing learners' needs;
- planning and preparing teaching and learning programmes for groups and individuals;
- developing and using a range of teaching and learning techniques;
- managing the learning process;
- providing learners with support;
- assessing the outcomes of learning and learners' achievements;
- reflecting upon and evaluating one's own performance and planning future practice;
- meeting professional requirements.

The Standards were further intended to enable colleges to adapt their appraisal systems and appropriate professional activities to meet the needs of all categories of teaching staff. What was needed to drive the staff development plans was individual college commitment to staff development by identifying staff needs, drawing up staff development plans, and motivating staff to play an active part in staff development.

The LSC, the government organisation that replaced the FEFC and TECs, asked colleges to set out their staff development plans and evaluate them for their effectiveness on an annual basis. This was reinforced by Baroness Blackstone (2000) in a speech to the FEFC's annual general meeting in which she stressed the importance of continuing professional development backed by the Standards Fund:

> Existing staff need continuing professional development. . . . Colleges need to assess these individual needs together with their own priorities as determined in their business planning. And they should have flexibility to determine continuing professional development activities as appropriate. . . .
>
> The way to take this forward will be for the LSC to require colleges to conduct an audit of the development needs of their staff as part of their self-assessment and development planning process . . . the audit will provide a basis for a college to develop an action plan that sets clear targets for development activities.

FENTO, sponsored by the FEFC and then the LSC, recognised that new and part-time staff required not only financial incentives but also in-house support to become successful lecturers. They therefore produced the *Mentoring towards Excellence* pack of guidance and materials for supporting the staff development process and staff involved in that development. The pack was sent to every college in England in 2002 and contained a section dealing with the 'Mentoring Process' in which they give advice for setting up a mentoring programme in a college. It has provided colleges with a possible model for action to meet the needs of their current staff and to potentially increase the effectiveness of their staff development programme.

Levers for the identification of staff development needs may come from government initiatives or new standards but they may now also come from the Office for Standards in Education (Ofsted) and the Adult Learning Inspectorate (ALI) inspection reports. Ofsted and ALI have their own standards for further education in The Common Inspection Framework for Inspecting post-16 Education and Training. The inspection of provision will be guided by seven key questions under three broad headings.

Achievement and standards

1   How well do learners achieve?

The quality of education and training

2   How effective are teaching, training and learning?
3   How are achievement and learning affected by resources?
4   How effective are the assessment and monitoring of learning?
5   How well do the programmes and courses meet the needs and interests of learners?
6   How well are learners guided and supported?

Leadership and management

7   How effective are leadership and management in raising achievement and supporting all learners?

After an inspection, colleges are required to draw up a post-inspection plan that sets out to overcome any weaknesses highlighted in their inspection. The idea is not to blame underachieving staff but to give them opportunities to improve their performance via a targeted staff development programme.

Systematic continuous professional development in further education is still not widespread. Martinez (1999) has suggested that this may be because there are too many initiatives to cope with in developmental terms:

> The pace of change itself creates barriers to improvement. If teachers are running hard to stay still, continuing professional development for improvements becomes problematic.

For the 2003/04 academic year the Standards Funds which ensured some semblance of professional development via its categories will be embedded largely within the national base funding rate for colleges, i.e. it will be a small percentage of the funding that makes up the funding formula for an individual learner. This means that it will not be an easily identified part of the total income of the college and it will be subject more to the discretion of principals and senior management teams as to what proportion of funding will be given to continuing professional development. It is to be hoped that we will not return to the time when 'CPD is viewed as a maintenance rather than an improvement activity' (Hughes, 1999). Alternatively, it may prove that spend on CPD will be evaluated more rigorously and point the way to an enhanced use of mentoring programmes:

> many organisations are instituting formal mentoring programmes as a cost-effective way to upgrade skills, enhance recruitment and retention, and increase job satisfaction.
>
> (Jossi, 1997)

Interest in coaching, mentoring and peer-networking

Schools

The national strategy for continuing professional development in schools in the UK (see DfES, 2001a, b, c, d; Harrison, 2001) strongly advocates the use of coaching, mentoring and peer-networking mechanisms to enhance teacher professional development and performance in schools. It suggests that mutual support for learning, the dissemination of good practices, the translation of teacher learning to pupil learning and the embedding of desirable change are among the potential benefits to be realised from the adoption of such mechanisms. The strategy emphasises the importance of teachers learning with and from other teachers, the importance of school support in improving teacher practices as a result of professional development and the encouragement of schools to become professional learning communities.

In particular, *Learning and Teaching: A Strategy for Professional Development* (DfES, 2001a) suggests that professional development is most likely to lead to successful changes in teachers' practice where development involves, among other elements:

coaching and feedback on their professional practice over a period of weeks and months. This is a particularly important element, and can be decisive in determining whether changes in practice survive.

The importance of teacher mutual support is also echoed in the current Code of Practice for Providers of Professional Development for Teachers (DfES, 2001b).

> Professional development for teachers and those who work with them in schools has been changing dramatically over recent years. Much of it comes from the support colleagues provide for each other formally and informally. Equally, planned development is needed for individuals, departments and whole schools to improve the quality of education. This too may be in the form of collegial learning within schools.

In addition, the Green Paper, *Schools: Building on Success* (DfEE, 2001b) suggests:

> Successful schools are always outward facing and committed to sharing best practice and seeking innovative thinking wherever they can find it. This vital process of networking and sharing knowledge is at the heart of teachers' professionalism because it involves both learning from what works and contributing to the pool of professional knowledge. We will continue to emphasize the value that can come from teachers learning from each other – through observing lessons, feedback, coaching and mentoring – which many teachers find the most effective way to improve their practice.

The national strategy for continuing professional development appears to draw upon the work of Joyce and Showers (1988) and Oldroyd and Hall (1988) which shows that engagement of coaching assists the translation of training into increased impact on job performance. However, the encouragement of teacher collaboration and mutual support in professional development is not new. For example, peer-coaching has been a feature of teacher professional development in the USA for many years, and has been seen as a means to effect and embed lasting improvements in professional practice (see Shalaway, 1985; Swafford *et al.*, 1997; Swafford, 1998). Peer-coaching within the USA has been defined by Robbins (1995) as:

> a confidential process through which two or more professional colleagues work together to reflect upon current practices; expand, refine and build new skills; share ideas; conduct action research; teach one another, or problem solve within the workplace.

The use of coaching to support teachers in improving their practice has also been explored in Holland. Veenman (1995) and Veenman *et al.* (1998a and 1998b) have studied the effect of coaching skills training on the efficacy of school counsellors, primary school teachers and school principals as coaches of teachers. Taking coaching as a form of in-class support used to provide teachers with feedback on their own practice as a means to stimulate self-reflection, it was found that coaching was generally perceived as positive by teachers, with the potential to improve professional practice. Against a background of increasing uncertainty regarding the efficacy of attending unsupported external courses as a means to raise performance and effect sustainable change (see Swafford, 1998; Rhodes and Houghton-Hill, 2000; Walker and Stott, 2000) and guided by emergent research and national strategy, school management teams in the UK are now invited to consider the adoption of professional development activities which embrace the mutual teacher support implicit in coaching, mentoring and peer-networking relationships.

Colleges

Colleges may have formal or informal mentoring programmes. The following statements are typical of those who have managed or participated in mentoring programmes.

Academics typically claim that informal mentoring is more advantageous for the mentee than formal mentoring, while the reverse is suggested by practitioners.

(Klasen and Clutterbuck, 2002)

Mentoring can be done by anyone, at any time, in almost any place. . . . It can be carried out informally as an element of friendship, or formally as part of a highly structured employee orientation programme.

(Shea, 2002)

Mentoring operates best within a programme. A mentoring programme operates best within a system.

(Portner, 2001)

Organisations are advised to develop cultures where spontaneous mentor relationships develop and are supported. Formal mentor relationships based on some choice of partner will broaden the number of employees who can access these programmes and realise their benefits.

(Lacey, 1999)

Just because a relationship has begun because a learner is assigned to a mentor in a structured programme, does not mean that the relationship cannot be developed informally.

(Lewis, 2000)

A formal programme may possess perceived organisational value, i.e. if it is a formal programme, perhaps as part of a staff development programme, it is likely to have a senior manager who is able to ensure that appropriate time and administrative resources are made available. It should also ensure that mentors are given the training they need to become mentors. This may be expressed as a formal recognition of their knowledge and skills as mentors via postgraduate awards in mentoring from an HEI.

Teacher mentors are only one version of mentoring that is taking place in the further education sector. There are also teachers mentoring students, students mentoring students, staff peer mentoring, external volunteer mentors for staff and for students, and community volunteer mentors for adults and younger learners. Most mentoring schemes appear to be for individuals (protégés) who are new to a programme or activity and/or to support them through the apparent complexity of their new environment. Mentoring may also take place to address under-performance or to enhance current performance.

What is the relationship between coaching, mentoring and peer-networking?

In seeking to establish the nature, benefits and demands of coaching, mentoring and peer-networking it is pertinent to examine both business as well as educational literature sources, as these mechanisms have frequently found prominence within the corporate learning armoury. Figure 1.1 shows an input–process–output model intended to relate the place of coaching, mentoring and peer-networking in supporting teacher professional learning, organisational improvement and teacher retention.

In essence, both coaching and mentoring are complex activities closely associated with the support of individual learning. Mentoring implies an extended relationship involving additional behaviour such as counselling and professional friendship (see Gardiner, 1998). Peer-networking implies the facility to work together productively with other colleagues so as to learn from them or with them. Successful networking relationships are at the heart of coaching and mentoring.

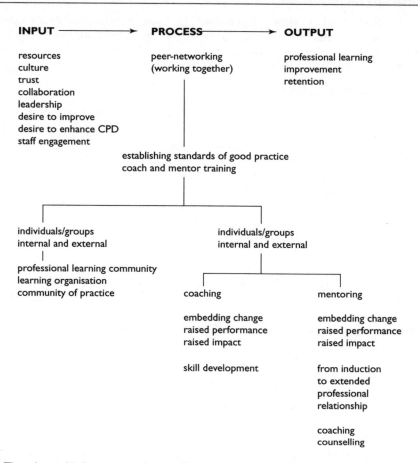

INPUT ⟶ **PROCESS** ⟶ **OUTPUT**

INPUT:
resources
culture
trust
collaboration
leadership
desire to improve
desire to enhance CPD
staff engagement

PROCESS:
peer-networking
(working together)

OUTPUT:
professional learning
improvement
retention

establishing standards of good practice
coach and mentor training

individuals/groups
internal and external

professional learning community
learning organisation
community of practice

individuals/groups
internal and external

coaching

embedding change
raised performance
raised impact

skill development

mentoring

embedding change
raised performance
raised impact

from induction
to extended
professional
relationship

coaching
counselling

Figure 1.1 The relationship between professional learning, organisational improvement and teacher retention through coaching, mentoring and peer-networking

How is coaching defined?

Professional development in some companies has drawn heavily on the development of openness, partnership and trust between individuals through the use of coaching (see Whitmore, 1995; Barker, 1998; Skiffington and Zeus, 2000):

> Coaching is unlocking a person's potential to maximize their own performance. It is helping them to learn rather than teaching them.
>
> (Whitmore, 1995)

> Coaching is a process that enables learning and development to occur and thus performance to improve.
>
> (Parsloe and Wray, 2000)

> Coaching is the art of facilitating the performance, learning and development of another.
> (Downey, 2001)

> Coaching is where you have a person observing you in your particular area of activity and commenting and feeding back on what you are doing well, strategies for improvement and so on, and then perhaps observing you again.
>
> (Harrison, 2001)

Joyce and Showers (1988) have argued that it is difficult to transfer teaching or management skills from professional development sessions to classroom settings without adequate support through coaching and the guidance of critical friends.

How is mentoring defined?

Professional development in some companies has drawn heavily on the development of openness, partnership and trust between individuals through the use of mentoring (see Parsloe, 1992; Beaumont, 1994; Parsloe and Wray, 2000) relationships:

> A mentor is a more experienced individual willing to share their knowledge with someone less experienced in a relationship of mutual trust. A mixture of parent and peer, the mentor's primary function is to be a transitional figure in an individual's development. Mentoring includes coaching, facilitating, counselling and networking.
>
> (Clutterbuck, 1991)

> Mentoring is a role which includes coaching, but also embraces broader counselling and support, such as career counselling, privileged access to information, etc.
>
> (Landsberg, 1996)

> Mentoring is when you talk to a more experienced colleague about things you want to do, about career opportunities.
>
> (Harrison, 2001)

> By becoming a mentor, you have the opportunity to affect the future if you share your ideals, your ethics and your professionalism.
>
> (Waugh, 2002)

> A mentor has the unique opportunity and privilege to encourage the professional and personal development of a colleague.
>
> (Dignard, 2002)

How is peer-networking defined?

Peer-networking may be taken as a generic term to encompass two or more individuals working together to enhance information exchange, dissemination of good practices, and the organisation of mutual support and learning. Such networking may occur between individuals or groups within individual organisations or in collaboration with other organisations. Networking between individuals is inherent in coaching and mentoring relationships.

A number of studies have explored peer-group collaboration and support as agents in raising teacher performance. For example, Ross and Regan (1993) found that listening to descriptions of professional experience had a positive effect on the growth of listeners who interacted with narrators. Moonen and Voogt (1998) found that using teacher networks to enhance professional development with respect to understanding and implementation of new information and communication technologies within school offered an enriched learning environment for participants. Smith (1999) reviewed the emergence of action-orientated 'peer support groups' as part of school-based professional development and argued for the importance of self-critical communities of teachers within schools aided by the establishment of a climate that is conducive to self-review and learning. In a study of secondary school teachers in Canada, Beatty (2000) suggested that collaborative reflection in teacher study groups may represent a powerful catalyst to professional growth and thus to the development of learning communities and organisational transformation. Day *et al.* (2002) have suggested that provision of opportunities for teachers to reflect on their teaching and engage in dialogue about it with other teachers can help to build motivation and commitment. The

National College for School Leadership (NCSL) in the UK has instituted the Networked Learning Communities programme in order to enhance learning from others and the dissemination of good practices. In networked learning communities, schools, teachers, pupils and leaders are intended to learn from each other and with each other. Learning in this way is intended to facilitate pupil learning, staff learning and professional development, leadership learning and leadership development, school-wide learning, school-to-school learning and network-to-network learning.

> Collaboration is a more powerful, more positive motivating force than competition. Networks are about schools working smarter together, rather than harder alone, to enhance learning at every level of the education system. Strong networks make it easier to create and share knowledge about what works in the classroom, to learn from each other's experiences, to find solutions to common problems. By working together in this way, networked schools are making professional practice visible and transferable.
>
> (NCSL, 2002)

Activity 1.6

Benchmarking collaboration

The potential benefits of coaching, mentoring and peer-networking activities within schools stem from the requirement for close partnership between colleagues within an environment of trust, safety, support and mutual respect. Here are three benchmarks for collaboration:

1   The culture of the organisation is denoted by individualism. Few teachers (a) share their practice with others, (b) work together to solve problems, and (c) there is only limited trust between colleagues.
2   The culture of the organisation shows sporadic collaboration and there are some instances where staff work together in an atmosphere of mutual trust.
3   The culture of the organisation is denoted by spontaneous collaboration. Staff work together freely and learn with and from each other. There is an established atmosphere of mutual trust and respect.

Where would you place your organisation with respect to these benchmarks? What action would be necessary to achieve benchmark 1, benchmark 2 or benchmark 3?

Extended activities

The remaining two 'extended' activities in this chapter are intended to further engage and challenge the reader with issues central to the exploration and development of an environment to sustain effective professional development. The first activity sets out to explore existing teacher development strategies within the reader's own professional context as a basis for further developments. The second activity enables readers to explore the possible establishment of coaching, mentoring and peer-networking as part of their own organisation's professional development environment.

Extended activity 1.7

An audit of teacher development strategies in your own organisation

Context

According to Law and Glover (1996), those schools which manage their professional development most effectively are those most frequently using five fundamental organisational elements in order to manage a secure and supportive professional development culture:

1   the effective management of information flows;
2   the development of shared and open planning processes;
3   the operation of clear resource allocation procedures with focused aims and targets;
4   the establishment of a clear evaluation strategy used as a basis for ongoing review and development;
5   the development of open networking opportunities to facilitate mutual support and reflection.

Professional development cultures will vary between schools and may either facilitate or hinder staff professional learning. What of the professional development culture in your own school or college? and what teacher development strategies are supported by it?

Four possible continuing professional development cultures may be identified when the interplay between leadership support for continuing professional development and staff commitment to it are taken into account.

Strong		
	A DIRECTIVE CULTURE • development as training • teachers viewed as 'trainees' • centrally imposed agenda • poor information flow • centralised and unclear resourcing	**A COLLABORATIVE CULTURE** • development well linked to needs • teachers viewed as 'professionals' • teachers participate in decision-making • networking opportunities available • resourcing to meet a range of needs
Leadership support for CPD	**A COMPLACENT CULTURE** • development imposed • teachers viewed as 'employees' • 'abdicated' decision-making • limited networking • poor information flow • limited or poor resourcing	**AN INDIVIDUALISED CULTURE** • development for self-improvement • teachers viewed as 'self-developers' • decisions influenced by micropolitics • informal and individualised networks • resourcing unclear or inadequate
Weak		

Low   High

Staff commitment to CPD

Source: Adapted from Law (1999)

Undertake an audit of teacher development strategies with your own organisation. How might the team/organisation be moved closer to a collaborative culture?

Aims

- To undertake an audit of professional development strategies within your team/organisation.
- To identify the prevailing professional development culture within your team/organisation.
- To suggest actions which would help move the team/organisation towards a more collaborative culture.
- To create a report for the Senior Management Team (SMT) based on your findings and suggestions.

Steps

This activity consists of three steps. Steps may be undertaken by individuals working alone or working in a group.

Step 1 involves undertaking an audit of professional development strategies within your team/organisation using the grid modified after Law (1999) so as to identify the prevailing professional development culture within your team/organisation.

Step 2 involves the formulation of actions to facilitate the movement of the team/organisation towards a more collaborative culture and concurrent identification of possible barriers to the actions proposed.

Step 3 involves the creation of a report for the SMT based on your findings and suggestions.

Step 1 Using the grid modified after Law (1999) please list facets of the professional development strategies identifiable within your team/organisation.

Directive	Collaborative	Complacent	Individualised

Which culture is most prevalent in your team/organisation?

continued

Step 2

Action required to move the team/organisation towards a more collaborative culture.

List each of the actions required to ensure greater collaboration and for each one, try and complete an action grid using the following format:

Action

Justification

Comment on likely impact upon pupils

Likely impact upon staff

Success criteria

Time scale

Staff

Resources

Monitoring

Evaluation

Other comments

Step 3

Create a report for the SMT based on your findings and action grids.

Extended Activity 1.8

A recognition of the role of coaching, mentoring and peer-networking in an organisation

Context

There are a number of opportunities to improve the overall performance of an organisation. This improvement occurs as a result of changes for the better in the way in which activities are modified. These modifications may be small or large and some are more important than others. Table 1 gives a list of potential changes that might face your organisation. As an organisation you need to determine the priorities for carrying out such changes.

Aims

- To identify the potential priorities in your organisation.
- To prioritise the actions required to improve your organisation in the future.
- To recognise the benefits of coaching, mentoring and peer-networking to your organisation.
- To determine the use of coaching, mentoring and peer-networking in your organisation.

Steps

This activity consists of three steps. The steps should be carried out as a series of group activities.

- *Step 1* invites the group to confirm the present and future challenges in your organisation.
- *Step 2* asks you to recognise and record the benefits of coaching, mentoring and peer-networking in your organisation.
- *Step 3* encourages your group to consider the links between the priorities and benefits. It also involves the group in identifying current examples of coaching, mentoring and peer-networking within your own organisation.

Step 1

As a management group use the following table to consider the current and future priorities of your organisation. Add other issues and priorities as necessary. Column 2 provides some questions of approach to assist you in determining your priorities.

Potential challenges/issues for your organisation	What are your organisation's current challenges/issues and what is your priority?		What are likely to be your organisation's future challenges/issues and what will be your priority?	
	Thoughts on the challenge/issue	Priority	Thoughts on the challenge/issue	Priority
To encourage the open and free flow of information	Do you have the results of a communication survey to build on?		Improvements sought?	
To provide an environment that promotes learning and the development of staff	Is the current budget for staff development as a proportion of the		Future measures of success?	

continued

Potential challenges/issues for your organisation	What are your organisation's current challenges/issues and what is your priority?	What are likely to be your organisation's future challenges/ issues and what will be your priority?
	organisations budget enough?	
Develop an organisation to enable the sharing of ideas and encourage innovation	Number of new developments this year vs. last year?	Will you set targets for developments?
Ensure all members of the organisation understand its mission and values and that they adhere to them	Do you know if staff really do understand and adhere?	Will you be changing your mission?
A regular turnover of staff	What is the turnover rate? Why is it taking place?	What improvement targets will you be seeking?
Have a high proportion of part-time staff	What is the proportion of part-time staff? Do you ensure they consider that they are part of the organisation?	Will you increase or decrease the number?
Seeking improvements in retention	Current retention rate and proposed improvement?	Future rates of retention?
Seeking improvements in achievement	Current achievement rates?	Future achievement targets?
Seeking to improve the performance of the workforce	What areas of performance are to be considered?	Performance indicators?
Develop leaders throughout the organisation	Is leadership distributed?	How will you empower?
Cost-effective running of the organisation	Best practice to be shared?	How will this be done?
Cost-efficient organisation	Where might costs be reduced?	How will this be managed?
Others		

Step 2

Using the following table, reflect on the benefits to an organisation of coaching, mentoring and peer-networking as listed below. Consider how these are taking place currently in your organisation.

Coaching	Mentoring	Peer-networking
A member of staff is seen as an 'expert'	The latent abilities of individuals are discovered and encouraged	Helps staff feel part of an organisation
Sharing of best practice	There is an improvement in the performance of staff	Improves communication
Staff who have received coaching conform to the recognised systems within the organisation	Staff are more likely to be retained	Shares best practice
Helps accelerate the learning curve of staff who are coached	Those who have been mentored rapidly grow in confidence	Encourages links across departments/teams
	Personal growth of the mentor and the learner	
	An increase in the mentor's and learner's awareness of their role in the organisation	
	An increase in their effectiveness in the organisation	
	Staff who have been mentored usually wish to act as mentors in the future – mentoring grows in the organisation	
	Strong working relationships	

Step 3

In your group(s) consider the links between your priorities in the first table and the benefits outlined in the second table. Reflect on the following questions and complete the table below. In which of the priorities may coaching, mentoring and peer-networking be useful forms of development?

Where might coaching, mentoring and peer mentoring be happening already within the organisation? Record examples you have identified and on which you might build.

Example C, M, PN	Description of activity

How might you modify your current practice to build on your current experiences of coaching, mentoring and peer-networking?

Chapter 2

Coaching, mentoring and peer-networking

Changing practice and raising standards

What are the benefits of coaching, mentoring and peer-networking?

Given a growing interest in coaching, mentoring and peer-networking as means to enhance professional development, the challenge associated with the successful management of these mechanisms emerges.

Despite a paucity of teacher collaboration in many organisations (see Harris, 2001), the encouragement of close partnerships between colleagues may help reduce or overcome any non-collaborative balkanisation (see Beatty, 2000) and yield some or all of the following benefits:

- The encouragement of collaboration may also be viewed as a tool of teacher empowerment. For example, Lieberman and Miller (2000) have suggested that teachers may well experience enhanced confidence and self-esteem through the mutual support offered by other colleagues.
- The engagement of support using coaching, mentoring and networking activities may assist in the transfer of teacher learning to pupil or student learning, resulting in greater impact within the classroom and the increased potential to raise standards and attainment (see Joyce and Showers, 1988; Oldroyd and Hall, 1988; Wallace, 1996; Swafford, 1998; Rhodes and Houghton-Hill, 2000).
- The locus of control of professional development may change beneficially, allowing teachers greater ownership of professional development and its potential impact, rather than professional development and change being seen as an imposition by others (see Whitmore,1995; Beatty, 2000; Downey, 2001).
- Enhanced individual, team and organisational performance may emerge by sharing and developing practice within an atmosphere of mutual trust and respect (see DfES, 2001a, b, c, d).

What difficulties are inherent in the management of coaching, mentoring and peer-networking?

Implementation of such mechanisms and the creation of an environment in which mutual support can flourish may present challenges within some organisations. For example, West-Burnham and O'Sullivan (1998) highlight the need for high-quality personal and interpersonal skills, mutual trust, confidence and respect within successful coaching relationships. However, it is known that collaboration between individuals so they can work and learn together is not prevalent in many organisations (see Harris, 2001). Close partnership and collaboration between colleagues is an important factor in enabling coaching, mentoring and peer-networking to flourish. In organisations where collaboration and trust between individuals is weak or not established, approaches to professional development which embrace these mechanisms have implications for leadership and management teams in those organisations. Clement and Vandenberghe (2001) have established the importance of collegial interactions between staff and particularly the role of school leaders in creating workplace conditions which allow learning opportunities and learning space for teachers, and so influence positively the professional development experience of teachers. Other important leadership and management issues relate to the acquisition and use of information and training, the careful selection of individuals as coaches and mentors, engaging staff commitment to a management style that incorporates coaching, mentoring and peer-networking, the use of accurate needs analysis and time constraints.

Teacher collaboration

The potential benefits of coaching, mentoring and peer-networking activities within organisations stem from the requirement for close partnership between colleagues within an environment of trust, safety, support and mutual respect (see Ponzio, 1987; Tharp and Gallimore, 1988; West-Burnham and O'Sullivan, 1998; Harris, 2000, 2001; Thompson, 2001). In organisations where the professional development culture already includes strong teacher collaboration, the adoption of coaching, mentoring and peer-networking should present fewer problems for staff. However, in many organisations it is known that teacher collaboration is not prevalent (Harris, 2001) and leadership and management intervention may be necessary to enable mutual teacher support to flourish.

Information and training

The paucity of information currently available in the UK concerning implementation issues, desirable working standards and the skill and training requirements of staff responsible for helping colleagues learn, needs to be addressed if the potential benefits of these mechanisms are to be realised. Nationally or internationally agreed guidance concerning good practices in coaching, mentoring and peer-networking in schools and colleges would be of use to teachers, leadership and management teams, trainers and others concerned with the raising of standards and attainment in schools and colleges.

Selection of individuals

The selection of coaches and mentors demands that individuals are sought who possess personal and professional qualities of the highest order (see West-Burnham and O'Sullivan, 1998). For example, insensitive and judgemental feedback regarding performance can damage learning relationships and encourage teachers to have negative views of their own abilities (Watkins and Whalley, 2000). In offering feedback, coaches and mentors would ideally have the potential to surpass the instrumental level of mechanistic direction for colleagues and would ideally foster opportunities to reflect deeply on practice. Thompson (2001) has suggested that coaching without reflection will not enable learning to take place, and West-Burnham and O'Sullivan (1998) point out that both coaching and reflection are required in order to produce a consolidated and internalised learning experience. Coaches and mentors are responsible for assisting the learning of colleagues who are adults, and with this goes the requirement to choose and train individuals who can sustain skills in enabling adults to learn. For example, Collarbone (2000) has identified that coaching requires the recognition that adults learn for specific purposes and that they must be motivated to want to learn. Discussing the mentoring of adults, Daloz (1998) identifies potential problems which may damage intended learning relationships between colleagues. It is suggested that problems could stem from differing ethics, possible misuse of power or excessive control, or from exaggerated emotional dependence by either party.

Engaging staff commitment

Approaches to professional development which ignore the issue of who is in control of the development are missing a vital component. Higgins and Leat (1997) point out that it is important to recognise that people are less likely to be receptive or positive with regard to professional development initiatives if they think they are being manipulated. Leadership and management teams need to consider how they will convince staff of the potential benefits of a management style which involves coaching, mentoring and peer-networking. For example, if the work of the coach or mentor becomes equated with only supervision due to weakness, staff may perceive an over-managerialist element rather than a true collaborative drive to support the learning of all teachers.

Needs analysis

In engaging coaching, mentoring or networking activities to support professional learning and teacher performance, leadership and management teams will need to carefully identify specific teacher learning needs in order to raise standards and attainment within their organisations. An accurate diagnosis of the causes of poor performance would enable better targeting of support and thus provide a more effective and efficient remediation to take place. This is illustrated by the work of Wragg (2000), who found that where poorly performing teachers did improve their performance, it was often because they had been given in-house support and a fellow teacher as mentor, which in turn had made an impact on their classroom teaching. Importantly, headteachers who had successfully pursued such a support strategy were able to make precise judgements about the nature of help needed.

Time constraints

Given severe time constraints in schools due to teacher workload (see Rhodes and Houghton-Hill, 2000; Thompson, 2001; GTC, 2002), leadership and management teams should consider how sufficient time may be created to allow the coach or mentor to undertake their role. This may be particularly problematic in schools where all staff are engaged in full-time class contact. It is reasonable to assume that staff in some schools and colleges may be reluctant to take on the additional responsibilities inherent in coaching and mentoring. Leadership and management teams may wish to consider the use of a consultant such as an LEA officer to undertake a coaching or mentoring role.

Each educational organisation has a unique context and an individual improvement journey to follow. Those organisations choosing to adopt coaching, mentoring or peer-networking mechanisms need to consider their position with respect to developing true collegiality. For example, some organisations may seek to develop towards a professional learning community (see Thompson, 2001), whereas others may adopt a more limited vision and employ these mechanisms strategically as quick fixes for immediate performance difficulties. Given that organisations spend significant sums of money on professional development with the intention of raising teacher performance (see Rhodes and Houghton-Hill, 2000; Rhodes, 2001), organisations actively seeking the potential benefits of coaching, mentoring and peer-networking relationships will also need to consider the placement of these mechanisms as part of normal working patterns in order to engender a climate of safety and trust.

Activity 2.1

Constraints to coaching, mentoring and peer-networking

Three separate perspectives are thought to influence professional development:

- the needs and aspirations of the individual;
- the needs and priorities of individual organisations;
- national priorities.

The engagement of peer-networking, coaching and mentoring relationships appears to offer potential benefits helping to serve the individual, the organisation and national priorities such as raising standards and attainment.

Drawing on the possible organisational constraints outlined in the text above, namely:

- collaboration;
- information and training;
- selection of individuals;
- engagement of staff commitment;
- needs analysis;
- time constraints,

make a rank order of these constraints with respect to your own organisation or team.

- Does your rank order agree with those of other colleagues?
- Is there a commonly held constraint within the organisation or team?
- Are there models within the organisation or team that could be adopted to minimise constraints?
- How are such constraints minimised in other organisations with which you have contact?
- What other sources of information might be sought to help minimise constraints?

Coaching as a process

Coaching represents a peer-networking interaction (working together) which draws upon collaboration and mutual trust. It is usually a short-term relationship which can be used to help embed change, raise performance, raise impact and assist in skill development. Good coaches will be active with the establishment of learners' needs, be sensitive to preferred learning styles and will ensure that the learner is able to engage in learning. These activities may be expressed as a series of steps:

- Ensure that learners are aware of their need to learn. This learning may concern the development of a new skill, a change in practice or an enhancement of performance.
- Assist in the development of a personal development plan in conjunction with the learner.
- Be involved in the implementation of the development plan.
- Ensure that evaluation is undertaken.

Activity 2.2

Dos and Don'ts of relationship-building skills

- Communicating to learners that they need to learn in order to make changes may be viewed as a threatening and potentially unwelcome intervention, even in organisations with some history of collegiality and collaboration.
- Make a list of dos and don'ts with respect to relationship-building skills. Remember that it is important that your colleague feels valued, worthwhile, understood and is prepared to trust you. It is important that you are personally prepared, respectful and non-judgemental.
- Compare your dos and don'ts with those of other colleagues.
- What general principles are emerging?

Activity 2.3

A personal development plan

It is important that learning is agreed and understood by both the learner and the coach. This is perhaps best expressed as a personal development plan.

The plan will typically offer clarity on:

- what is to be learned in terms of an objective(s) or a target(s);
- what actions will need to be taken;
- when will it start;
- when will it end;
- what are the success criteria;
- how does this link to organisational, personal, national priorities;
- who else might be involved;
- are particular resources required;
- how will monitoring and evaluation take place;
- who will agree the plan.

Design a personal development plan for yourself with respect to a desired objective or target. Would your plan be suitable for a learner whom you were coaching?

Activity 2.4

Coaching style

To implement the plan you will need to apply your own coaching style to support the learner. Your style may be more hands-on or hands-off; however, your support will certainly call upon the need to provide feedback, to engage in active listening, pay attention to the needs of an adult learner, offer good questioning skills and an ability to confer constructive criticism if this is required.

Try and identify individuals within the organisation whom you may be called upon to coach. Would your style be more 'hands-on' or 'hands-off' with each of the individuals whom you have identified?

- Why do you think you may need to vary your style?
- What elements of your style would be common to all individuals?
- What elements might you choose to vary?

Finally, monitoring and evaluation to assess the success of the personal development plan is essential. Has learning taken place as required, was it cost-effective, what went right, what went wrong? What should happen next?

Mentoring as a process

Mentoring also represents a peer-networking interaction (working together) which draws upon collaboration and mutual trust. It is usually a longer term relationship which can be used to support individuals or groups to embed change, improve performance, raise impact and assist in personal and professional development. Mentoring may be used to support individuals through a combination of coaching and counselling from induction through to extended professional relationships. While coaching is an enabling and helping process, mentoring is essentially a supportive process. The mentor requires many of the same skills as a coach. Typical mentoring activities are outlined below as a series of steps.

Contribute to the development of self-awareness in the learner

A mentor can contribute at any stage in the preparation of a personal development plan. The mentor role is to be sensitive to and supportive of all the circumstances in which the learner is operating. Although the mentor may or may not be directly responsible for the learner's performance, the mentor has a role to play in developing self-awareness in the learner. The mentor is a source of support to learners in the achievement of their aspirations.

Support learners in managing their own learning

A mentor uses greater experience and supports the learner to think ahead in an atmosphere of trust and confidentiality. The mentor is a sounding-board on which the learner can draw. The mentor may meet regularly with the learner during the period of a personal development plan in order to offer advice. A good mentor will maintain and enhance the confidence of the learner in the workplace so that learning may take place.

Assist in evaluation

A mentor should provide non-judgemental feedback so that the learner may become reflective and be open to discussion about learning opportunities as well as potential barriers to their learning. The mentor can support the learner in self-evaluation against appropriate performance standards.

Training coaches and mentors to identify the appropriate standard

In order to play their part in enabling, helping and supporting learners, coaches and mentors should be cognisant of internally or externally set performance standards which learners are attempting to meet. In schools, standards may be associated with internal development planning or in relation to the standards set by external agencies such as Ofsted, the DfES or the TTA. The use of standards provides a particular dilemma in FE, since it is not clear which standards should be used as the goal. There are several sets of standards that may be followed, although a combination of them, while complex, may be the most appropriate.

The first standards to consider might be those of Ofsted/ALI (2001) as set out in the Common Inspection Framework. These are the standards against which a college will be judged publicly and yet they are standards based on criteria that do not in all cases have absolute definition. The standards are set within a framework of criteria around seven questions concerned with teaching and learning and their leadership and management. Within this framework, the quality of teaching is judged against a range of standards graded from 1 to 7. Any coach or mentor should be aiming towards the goal of achieving and maintaining a Grade 1–2, the very good or excellent teacher, both for themselves and for the learners they help and support.

A second set of standards is provided by FENTO (2000). FENTO has produced a set of standards for teaching and supporting learning in further education in England and Wales. The standards are based on the assumption that those who teach in the sector already possess specialised subject knowledge, skills and experience. The standards, therefore, address the professional development of teachers and teaching teams rather than the development of their subject expertise. The standards flow from the key purpose of the teacher which FENTO defines as:

The key purpose of the FE teacher and those directly involved in supporting learning is to provide high-quality teaching, to create effective opportunities for learning and to enable all learners to achieve to the best of their ability.

The FENTO standards will be required for those responsible for mentoring trainee teachers in FE; however, when mentoring more experienced teachers it is likely that the Ofsted standards will be more appropriate.

There may be a third standard that would be set by the college quality assurance guidelines based on their own observation practices. For example, some colleges have set out to identify and promote excellent teaching staff as 'advanced practitioners' and to designate them as coaches or mentors to help improve the standard of teaching. These advanced practitioners would use their own standards of teaching as models to be achieved by their colleagues.

There may be a fourth standard, the Investors in People Standard, which ensures that the college as a whole is committed to developing its workforce in order to achieve its aims and objectives.

Coaches and mentors should provide the critical and safe environment in which the learner may learn and be involved in judging themselves against appropriate standards. As suggested above, coaches may use the standards and information from their learners differently than they would if they were acting as a mentor.

Pegg (1999) suggests that good coaches often take three steps:

1   They encourage people to build on their strengths.
2   They equip people to tackle areas for improvement.
3   They enable people to achieve ongoing success.

Not all researchers agree on the three steps, but they do see coaching as a more structured and direct approach to working with others than that of a mentor.

In the case of mentoring, Lewis (2000) suggests a three-stage process which he calls the 3D approach: Define, Describe, Decide. For example:

- Define what it is that you want to change.
- Describe accurately what you are trying to do in making that change.
- Decide how you are going to carry out the activity and how you will judge its success.

Coaching is always part of mentoring, but coaching does not always involve mentoring. Coaching within the context of a mentoring relationship has to do with the skill of helping an individual fill a particular knowledge gap by learning how to do things more effectively. Steps to achieving an agreed standard will rely on recognising what is the standard to be achieved and recognition of the standard and the distance the learner has to travel for that achievement.

Activity 2.5

Identifying appropriate standards

Train coaches and mentors to identify the appropriate standard.
   With a group of established or potential coaches and mentors take the following steps:

- In small groups ask them to define good teaching by using a series of bullet points. Write the bullet points on flipcharts.
- Review the responses as a whole group and discuss until there is an acceptable agreement over the definition.

- Ask them to compare their definition to an external standard such as the Ofsted framework and add to the definition if necessary.
- As a whole group ask them to decide how they would use the information they have now gathered in their role as coaches or mentors. What steps would they take with respect to conveying the required standard to their learner? What documentation would they make available to their learner?
- Ask the whole group to come to a common agreement on what steps they would take to convey the required standard to their learner and what documentation should be available to their learner?

Observing a learner in the classroom or workshop and giving feedback

Having an agreed standard will help both the coach or mentor and their learners to identify their priorities. Change is an important reason for introducing a coaching or mentoring programme. It is likely that an important part of that change process will occur within the classroom or workshop. Recognising the current practice in the classroom or workshop will be a function of the relationship between the coach or mentor and their learner. Carrying out an observation of the learner in the classroom or workshop is the most informative way of determining current practice. However, there are some drawbacks, since some schools and colleges carry out the observation of lessons as part of their quality assurance procedures, and as a result staff are likely to be familiar with the formal, judgemental approach to observation.

The mentoring relationship in particular is non-judgemental and offers support before, during and after an observed session. If a mentor is to be engaged in an observation, this will usually occur after the mentor and learner have met and understood the nature of mentoring and the role of the mentor.

Activity 2.6

The Johari Window in establishing a supportive relationship

In establishing a supportive relationship the learner and mentor may wish to consider the use of the Johari Window to help them get to know one another better.

First, the mentor should complete the windows with as much information about themselves as they wish. The mentor should at least attempt windows A and C. The learner may then be invited to complete the windows. Information may be added to as the relationship develops and other windows, such as window B, may be completed.

	Known to self	Not known to self
Known to others	*Public area* A	*Blind spot* B
Not known to others	*Private area* C	*Unknown* D

Observation by a mentor has to be in the gift of the learner and requires three steps.

Pre-observation

'Observations themselves are more likely to be successful if both parties contribute to making the experience constructive' (Ewans, 2001). The mentor and learner decide what is to be observed and how it will be observed and what they will hope to gain from the observation. The mentor will listen to the requirements of the learner and may use records from previous 'quality assurance' observations as a starting point for their dialogue. For example, from Butcher (2002): 'My mentor selected areas to enable me to draw on my background in marketing – and Elizabethan poetry – to help me feel confident, so I think that was really supportive of her.'

Observation

The mentor and learner decide how the observation is to be recorded using the appropriate paperwork. The mentor will usually record in a preferred style. The records should enable the mentor to feed back accurately and with clear evidence for any comments. Montgomery (1999) recommends the use of a sampling frame to record classroom observations as it enables the production of 'a naturalistic record involving rapid writing of factual events as they occur'.

Post-observation

The mentor and the learner decide how information gained from the observation will be fed back and what will be done with the results of the feedback. Ewans (2001) agrees with the importance of feedback: 'Feedback should generally be an affirming and encouraging process.' There are at least two schools of thought as to when to give feedback: (1) those who suggest feedback immediately after the lesson, and (2) those who give feedback at an agreed time and place at least one day after the observation. In (1) the session is fresh in their minds and instant recall will help in the formative assessment process. Learners may be over- or underwhelmed by their performance and may not reflect accurately on their performance, and may not be ready to listen or respond to their mentor's comments. There may be the need for some instant reassurance about the performance to give learners some peace of mind or to enable them to celebrate their achievements. Ewans (2001) offers support to this approach in stating: 'It should happen soon after the observation, when the teaching and learning are fresh in the minds [of mentor and learner].' Whereas (2) gives both the learner and the mentor time to consider what they have seen and to provide a more thorough response to what was observed. Mentors will also have had time to think about how they will present their comments and perhaps draw up some sort of priority of what was observed. Beels and Powell (1994) state:

> It is important that you are honest – it is equally important that – where an observed lesson has been, in the new teacher's words, 'a disaster' – your sensitivity means that you will weigh up how much you need to say.

For the learners, it may give them time to consider what actions might be appropriate as a result of their performance. However, it may allow the learners to reflect too deeply on their performance and be over-critical during the feedback.

The post-observation feedback is a vital form of professional development for both the mentor and the learner. It should be managed by the learner in order to remain non-threatening. It is usual for mentors to ask learners what they thought about the session and any specific points they were seeking to improve.

> A good mentor is someone who can guide and discuss – ask the [learner] what they think rather than just telling you. . . . Anyway it feels like less of a criticism if you realise for yourself what is wrong.
>
> (Maynard, 2000)

The mentor may then adopt the 'sandwich approach' and find elements of the observation to praise, followed by an element to be criticised, followed by an element to be praised. 'I usually start by asking her how she feels . . . I wouldn't dream of dictating something . . . as a mentor you have to treat these[learners] with respect' (Butcher, 2002).

Some mentors may consider that this form of feedback is inappropriate, as the receiver only listens to the first item of praise and ignores the criticism. They would advocate a more coaching form of feedback in which learners would identify their 'weakness', which would be confirmed and clearly described in discussion with the learner. The learner would then draw up a picture of what should have been done, with the guidance of the mentor. Mentors are likely to show empathy by offering examples from their own experiences of similar actions, or by offering stories from other people's experiences. The learner would then work out what action should be taken to overcome the 'weakness' and then write up those actions as part of an individual learning plan. This is likely to form the basis of the next observation session.

Extended activities

The remaining two 'extended' activities in this chapter are intended to further engage and challenge the reader with issues central to successful coaching, mentoring and peer-networking. The first activity sets out to explore the essential skill of feedback within the coaching and mentoring relationship. The second activity enables the reader to further explore how staff networking, coaches and mentors can raise the effectiveness of professional development within their own organisation.

Extended activity 2.7

Planning for effective feedback

Context

Those selected to act as coaches or mentors will find themselves continually having to give feedback. Inexperienced learners may want to ask, *'How am I doing?'*; more experienced learners may ask, *'If I do it this way do you think that it will be better?'* Feedback provides learners with important information about how their behaviour is perceived by others. Effective feedback is essential to learning by increasing awareness of both what individuals are doing and how they are doing it.

Learners are motivated when their contribution is recognised, and feedback which includes praise can encourage development. Where constructive criticism of performance is required, it is important that this is done in such a way as to avoid resentment on the part of the recipient. For example, insensitive and judgemental feedback regarding performance can damage learning relationships and encourage teachers to have negative views of their abilities, which in turn could lead to lower standards (Watkins and Whalley, 2000). There are many factors which impinge upon the effectiveness of feedback, such as lack of mutual trust, power relationships and the structure of the feedback provided. Providing effective feedback for adult colleagues, which will enable them to reflect and learn from their strengths and weaknesses, presents a challenge which many people will try to avoid. For example:

- 'It's not part of my job';
- 'I don't have time';
- 'I don't have enough information';
- 'Who am I to judge others?';
- 'it will damage our relationship'.

continued

However, it is essential that coaches and mentors develop skills associated with provision of effective feedback if they are to support the learning of others. Helpful tips on giving effective feedback are provided by Parsloe and Wray (2000). The following has been modified from the list that these writers provide:

- be sensitive to the fact that you are providing feedback for adults;
- make feedback honest, and balance positive and negative messages;
- think about the tone and language you will use;
- try and be descriptive rather than appearing judgemental;
- prepare your feedback in advance of your meeting;
- act as a good role model and guide the recipient to reflect upon action to be taken as a result of your feedback.

Aims

- To comment critically upon the feedback of others.
- To experience the preparation of feedback.
- To experience the provision of feedback.
- To reflect upon the effectiveness of your feedback.
- To plan ways in which to improve the effectiveness of your feedback.

Steps

This activity consists of five steps. All steps (except step 3) may be undertaken by individuals working alone; however, engagement in the discussion generated by working with others is recommended wherever possible.

- *Step 1* involves commenting critically on a feedback transcript by drawing on examples of good and poor practices described in this text.
- *Step 2* invites preparation of feedback either as a result of gaining the agreement of a colleague to observe their lesson or by watching a videotaped lesson.
- *Step 3* invites presentation of your feedback to the colleague whose lesson you observed, or presenting and sharing your feedback with others who watched a videotaped lesson with you.
- *Step 4* requires critical reflection upon the feedback you have prepared/presented so as to identify strengths and weaknesses.
- *Step 5* invites action planning in order to improve the effectiveness of your feedback.

Step 1

The following text represents a transcript of a section of feedback offered by one teacher to another teaching colleague. The feedback results from a thirty-minute observation of a GCSE science lesson. Please identify any strengths and weaknesses in the feedback provided and list them in the boxes provided. If possible, compare your responses with those of other colleagues. What are the areas of agreement and disagreement and why?

The practical demonstration you did at the front was good but you were rather poor at organising access to chemicals when the students were doing their own investigation. You seriously need to consider this point. I would have had team leaders from each group coming out to collect all that was needed. Have you considered asking the laboratory technician to help you with a better organisation? What do you think went well in the lesson? Why was this? I thought that some pupils were really engaged in the task, what did you think? How might you go about engaging all the pupils? I hope that you will continue with the good work that you did but please don't let them all run to the front in future.

Strengths	Weaknesses

Step 2

Agree with a colleague to observe a lesson or watch, with other colleagues if possible, a videotape of a lesson. Prepare for a ten-minute feedback for your colleague or to share with your group based on the observations made. Please use the following headings to guide comments you will make. Be sure to provide feedback which is effective and will contain learning points for the recipient. Use only specific items emerging from your observations and avoid going beyond the evidence presented to you. Please use the following headings to guide comments you will make:

- expectations set by the teacher;
- planning;
- methods and strategies used;
- classroom relationship management;
- classroom discipline;
- assessment;
- lesson flow ;
- time on task;
- use of homework;
- time and resource management.

Step 3

Having drafted out a content and structure (order) of your ten-minute feedback, please offer this to your colleague or share it with your group. Collect comments from recipients of your feedback and listen carefully to their response to your feedback. Did you include any learning points? Did recipients feel positive or negative about your feedback? Please note the key points.

continued

Step 4

Please identify any strengths and weaknesses in your feedback and list them like this.

Strengths	Weaknesses

Please complete the following. I could improve my feedback by:

Objective 1 ....

Objective 2 ....

Objective 3 ....

Objective 4 ....

Objective 5 ....

Step 5

Finally, prepare an action plan to ensure that objectives you have identified in Step 4 are taken through to achievement. If possible, engage the support of colleagues in the formulation of your action plan.

Objective	Action required	By whom	Resources required	Success criteria	Complete by

Extended activity 2.8

Raising the effectiveness of professional development

Context

Harris *et al.* (2001) suggest that effective professional development for subject leaders which generates awareness, knowledge, understanding and behaviour development is least likely to occur in short courses and most likely to occur in long partnership and school-based models. Within such partnership and school-based models of professional development, a number of common elements were found to emerge:

- an emphasis upon collaboration;
- involvement and support of senior management;
- flexibility and intermittent training points;
- external agency;
- context-related planning and development;
- necessity of enquiry and reflection;
- use of research to inform practice;
- evaluation and data analysis.

Taking these elements to concur with DfES (2001e) guidance on effective professional development for all teachers, how might the effectiveness and good value of professional development be improved by the activity of coaches and mentors within your own professional context?

Aims

- To identify barriers to the transmission of teacher learning to pupil or student learning.
- To identify barriers to impact which may be overcome by the deployment of staff networking, coaching or mentoring so as to enhance the impact of professional development within the organisation.
- To comment critically on current organisational staff development policy in the light of your findings.
- To assess value for money obtained with respect to current approaches to professional development within the organisation.

Steps

This activity consists of four steps. Steps may be undertaken by individuals working alone or in a group.

- *Step 1* involves identification of possible barriers within the organisation to the transmission of teacher learning to pupil/student learning.
- *Step 2* involves reflection on the barriers to impact identified so as to facilitate identification of additional support to enhance the impact of professional development.
- *Step 3* involves critical comment upon current organisational staff development policy.
- *Step 4* involves an assessment of value for money obtained resulting from current protocols of professional development within the organisation.

continued

Step 1

The following list represents a hypothetical model of staff development procedures within an organisation intended to lead to raised standards and attainment. In reality, the steps involved may assist or impede the transmission of teacher learning to classroom impact for pupils/students.

- development planning;
- professional development requirement identified;
- choice of development;
- quality of professional development attended;
- degree of motivation of attendee(s);
- attendee learning;
- school dissemination mechanisms;
- staff collaboration;
- support for further development leading to embedding in practice;
- new practice as a result of development activity;
- monitoring and evaluation of impact;
- raised attainment for pupils/students.

Step 2

Make a list of the barriers identified, and by drawing on the text in this chapter try and identify where staff networking, coaching or mentoring might help overcome those barriers and so enhance the impact of professional development in the classroom experience of pupils/students. Set out your list like this.

Barrier identified	Deployment of staff networking? Coaching? or mentoring?	Expected improvement?

Step 3

Obtain and comment critically on the school or college staff development policy. In the light of the above findings, is policy adequate to ensure the transmission of teacher learning to pupil/student learning? Could it be improved?

Step 4

Given that the concept of value for money consists of economy, efficiency and effectiveness, draw upon your responses to the first three steps in this activity and provide a short written statement for the senior management team which enables judgement on the value for money obtained with respect to current professional development protocols within the organisation, and whether greater value for money could be obtained by the deployment of staff networking, coaching or mentoring.

Chapter 3

Developing coaching, mentoring and peer-networking in your own organisation

Needs analysis to best practices

Introduction

An organisation has to consider why it should set up a coaching or mentoring programme and how this programme should be operated. There is a growing body of evidence which shows the success of coaching and mentoring programmes, but little comment about failure. Organisations may decide to introduce programmes with significantly different foci. For example, there are those schemes that use mentoring or coaching as remediation for improving the quality of teaching and learning. Other schemes use coaching or mentoring in support of classroom observation to improve teaching and to recognise and share good practice in preparation for a forthcoming inspection. There is a growing number of schemes in schools and colleges for the development and improvement of leaders and managers. There are those schemes that use mentoring to support the development of teachers who are new to the organisation. Fabian and Simpson (2002) have researched the benefits of mentoring support for a new teacher to a school or college and concluded that new staff can be helped to make sense of, and understand, the uncertainties they face and the insecurities they feel. Wendell (1997) has also provided evidence to support the notion that mentoring is important for new staff to settle into new surroundings.

On determining what scheme may be beneficial, organisations need to determine who should act as coaches or mentors. Recent developments in colleges have enabled them to set up advanced practitioner posts for those staff who excel at teaching. In giving such staff the role of mentors they hope to share their experience and good practice across the institution. Others have set up posts of college mentor to be responsible for the support of new part-time staff, and this support will include induction, ongoing point of contact and observation to assist in the improvement of teaching.

The one element which all these schemes have in common is that they are formal, and thus require the support and recognition of senior management teams in their organisation. Such support and recognition is important in the long-term maintenance of any scheme. This view is reinforced by Kibby (2003):

> Any CEO or manager truly interested in change and/or improving workforce performance must also become deeply committed to the mentoring process. . . . A mentor is a valuable tool for developing a personal investment in change and a commitment to it whilst supporting the individual through the fear, into the risk taking and then finally on to acting.

Research does suggest that there are benefits in having informal schemes, but for the overall development of staff in a school or college the chance element of an informal approach has to be overcome. A formal scheme requires a framework within which coaching and mentoring may take place. The elements of a typical formal scheme are:

* The aims of the scheme (reflecting the vision of the organisation).
* The objectives of the scheme (clear outcomes for the scheme that are measurable within specified time frames).

- The roles and responsibilities of coaches and mentors.
- The selection process for coaches and mentors.
- The training of coaches and mentors.
- The elements of the coaching and mentoring process.
- The management and monitoring of the scheme.
- The review and evaluation of the scheme.

The appointment and training of coaches and mentors

In seeking to train or appoint coaches or mentors, the organisation needs to be clear about the purpose of the coaching or mentoring sought. Are there coaches and mentors already at work within your organisation? Does the organisation have a policy to guide their work?

Activity 3.1

Coaching and mentoring in your own organisation

- Establish if coaching and/or mentoring already takes place within your organisation.
- Define a role for coaches and/or mentors within your organisation.
- Define the management of coaches and/or mentors within your organisation.
- Define a policy for coaching and/or mentoring within your organisation.

A checklist

Which staff?

Whatever the method for selection, it should be clearly stated and all the staff in the organisation should be aware of the criteria for selection. However, should any member of staff be allowed to become a coach or mentor? Should only staff of a particular status or qualification or experience be selected as coaches or mentors? Will managers be allowed to be mentors? Brown (2001) suggests that becoming a mentor has tended to be seen as a reflection of seniority and experience. However, there is growing support in the literature for a move away from hierarchical relationships towards a search for mutuality, of two-way communication in the mentoring role, sometimes expressed as a *buddy role* for the mentor. Most schemes either identify expert teachers to be coaches or mentors or ask for volunteers. Some draw up a 'job description' and interview formally for the role. Most staff will have some idea of what a coach or mentor might be or do before they consider the role. The following definition of mentoring is one of the most succinct found in the literature: 'the act of helping another learn' (Bell, 2002). This also identifies the complexity of the role, as how do you help someone else to learn?

Consider time constraints

What will be the specific time allocated by the college or school for the coaching or mentoring role, given the paperwork involved in developing and interacting with the learners' personal development plan and the learners themselves. How long will the scheme be in operation? Time will be required for meetings along with specific private places for the meetings to ensure confidentiality. It is desirable that the coach or mentor maintains a record of the meeting so that each meeting may have an outcome and some formative assessment with respect to the personal development plan. Agreed action may be formulated at the end of each meeting. Experience has shown that action ideas may be proposed at the meeting and the learner allowed a few days in which to draw up an action plan and give it to the coach or mentor. The action plan should have milestones which would form the basis of future meetings. Meetings should help the growth of the relationship between the coach or mentor and the learner. What time will be allowed for monitoring and evaluating the outcomes of the scheme?

Matching the coach or mentor to the learner

This matching could be a voluntary process or made to be a compulsory process. If voluntary, then coaches and mentors and potential learners should provide a profile of their experience, interests and aims for being in the scheme and then those with 'like' profiles should be paired off. This method is time-consuming, and may require someone with the wisdom of Solomon to make the matches. If the scheme is voluntary then the coach, the mentor or the learner may leave the scheme at any point and thus a lot of preparation time may be felt to be wasted. If compulsory, then coaches and mentors are allocated a learner and 'told to get on with it'! They should still have the option of stepping away from the partnership if it is not working. Schemes may also consider a strategy to develop active cross-departmental/organisational partnerships.

A learning contract?

Some schemes may use a learning contract. This may be a written contract or a verbal contract that is agreed at the first meeting. One of the important items would be the confidentiality of the meetings. Some schemes ask for coaching or mentoring reports, which may of course limit the trust of the learner in the reasons for the scheme. The contract should also point out the flexibility and length of the scheme. The contract may also identify the approach of the coach or mentor. At the conclusion of the relationship, the contract may include a meaningful way to celebrate success and a comfortable way to move on.

Training before the scheme begins

All coaches and mentors should receive training before the scheme begins in order to understand the scheme and the boundaries or limits of the scheme. They should have the opportunity to confirm their wish to become coaches or mentors, recognise their skills, develop those skills and have the chance to develop a network with other coaches and mentors who share common values.

Skills in the field of human relations

In the previous chapter, coaching and mentoring were seen to be similar processes, both relying on networking and collaboration between colleagues, but also exhibiting some differences in the nature of the relationship between the coach, the mentor and the learner. Some of the key sub-processes in these relationships are:

- establish learners' needs;
- take account of preferred learning style;
- ensure that learning is engaging for the learner;
- assist in the removal of barriers to learning;
- help maintain learner motivation;
- monitor and evaluate performance against the personal development plan.

The first stage of any training programme for mentors or coaches is to know their fellow participants. This is a group to whom they may well refer for support and advice as the scheme progresses.

At an early stage in any coaching or mentoring programme it is important for the prospective coach or mentor to find out what is expected of them and whether they feel they are able to meet those expectations.

Activity 3.2

Getting to know your fellow coaches or mentors – ice-breakers

- Using a name tag, draw a picture to represent your name and invite your colleagues to guess your name from the drawing.
- Line up in distance travelled to attend the training session.
- Line up in birthday month order.
- Line up in length of time you have worked in the organisation.
- Without speaking, line up in alphabetical order – have you remembered names?

Activity 3.3

Learner requirements and the attributes of coaches and mentors

In small groups make a list of what a learner requires from a coach or mentor. Compare your list with other groups. Did you agree? What was missing?

What attributes does a coach or mentor need to have in order to meet your agreed list of leaner requirements? Compare your list with other groups. Did you agree? What was missing?

Using your agreed list of attributes, say whether you feel you have these attributes, need to develop them further or need to develop them for the first time.

If prospective coaches and mentors have limited numbers of the attributes it does not rule them out, but helps them recognise what they have to do. The following exercise may be more comforting and informative.

Activity 3.4

An iceberg activity

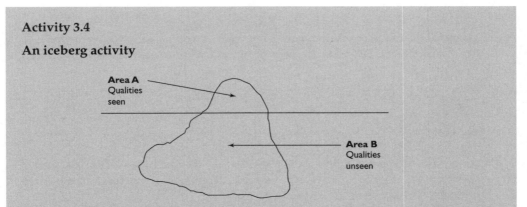

Area A
Qualities
seen

Area B
Qualities
unseen

Your life experiences are rather like an iceberg. What anyone can see when they look at you is probably one-eighth of your capability.

In Area A list those qualities and experiences that you think people see when they meet you for the first time.

In Area B list those qualities and experiences that you know you have gained over your lifetime but may not be obvious.

Share this information with a colleague – any surprises?

Source: Adapted from Malderez and Bodoczky (1996)

The Iceberg activity has helped you identify the whole of that experience that as a coach or mentor it will be vital to draw on to use with your learner. Remember that your learners too will have their own iceberg, and much of their experience and many of their qualities may need uncovering in order to use them to the full. Bell (2002) offers other ways of 'measuring' yourself to determine if you are capable of being a mentor. He considers that there are particular attributes which people bring to the mentoring process that would be useful if they understood how these might be used. For example, are you a person who is open with their feelings and finds it easy to trust others? Will a learner find that openness helpful or overbearing or intimidating?

Activity 3.5

What do I bring to being a coach or mentor?

Step 1
On your own.
Who is the most influential person I know, i.e. someone who impacted on my behaviour, the way I work or live my life.
What qualities did they have that brought about this influence? List them.

Step 2
Share the list with a colleague.
Were your experiences similar, were there similar characteristics in the influential person?
Working together, are there any messages for you as future coaches or mentors? List them.

Step 3
Compare and share your coach or mentor message with the rest of the group.
Then as a group list the messages on a flip chart sheet. Discuss how as coaches and mentors you might make use of these messages.

It is clear that the role of coach or mentor is one which needs to take into account the learning needs of the learner, and therefore an ability to engage with a learning needs analysis is a vital skill.

Activity 3.6

A needs analysis

Coaches and mentors need considerable skills in the field of human relations. All coaches and mentors need to take into account learning needs of learners, and hence learning needs analysis represents a vital skill.

Undertake a learning needs analysis with a colleague, using some or all of the suggested standards for coaches and mentors in this book (see Chapter 7, p. 93).

Performance requirements (may be defined by standards)	–	Present actual performance	=	Area for performance development (the sum of individual teacher learning needs)

Try and complete the following pro forma with the help of a colleague.

Area of performance
to be discussed:

Required level of
performance:

Present level of
performance:

Area for performance
development:

Suggested professional learning/
training required to bridge
performance gap:

Any other comments:

The role of coach or mentor will be demanding and time-consuming, but it will also be very rewarding.

The benefits of coaching and mentoring for the coach or mentor

Ragins and Cotton (1999) have identified benefits derived by the mentor as well as by the learner as a result of the mentoring process; for example, a broader understanding of their organisation, credibility in the eyes of their colleagues, patience, risk-taking, appreciation of cultural differences, revealing the best in others. There are also benefits for coaches and mentors in terms of developing their own reflectivity. For example, Butler and Chao (2001) have recognised that for mentors, one of the benefits was that it helps them to think more about teaching and learning issues, thus making them more aware of their own learning styles. As a result, they are better able to formulate effective learning strategies. The more reflective and self-aware the mentors become about teaching and learning, the more effective they are in supporting their learner.

Extended activities

The remaining two 'extended' activities in this chapter are intended to further engage and challenge the reader with issues central to successful coaching, mentoring and peer-networking. The first activity sets out to explore further the necessary attributes of a coach or mentor. The second activity enables the reader to experiment with a coach or mentor partnership.

Extended Activity 3.7

Preferred working style: recognising your own attributes and abilities

Context

Do you have the attributes necessary to be a coach or a mentor? There is no clear agreement on what are the most appropriate attributes, but what is important is that the coach or mentor recognise their own attributes in order to work to their strengths for the benefit of the learner.

Aims

- To explore your own preferred working style.
- To explore and judge your abilities as a mentor.

Steps

This activity consists of two steps. Steps may be undertaken by individuals working alone, but working in pairs is preferable as you are required to share findings with a colleague in order to help assess the implications of your findings.

- *Step 1* involves undertaking an audit of your preferred style of working and offers the opportunity to reflect upon how you might develop your non-preferred styles.
- *Step 2* involves completing a mentor-scale audit so as to explore your mentoring abilities in terms of 'sociability', 'dominance' and openness'.

Step 1

Preferred style of working.

In pairs consider the following words. Tick the four words that you consider closely describe your approach to life.

Intuitive (I)	Planner (L)	Sharing (E)	Impulsive (E)
Experimenter (P)	Improviser (I)	Questioning (P)	Control (L)
Animated (E)	Emotional (E)	Deliberate (L)	Vision (I)
Reserved (L)	Factual (P)	Casual (I)	Analyse (L)
Reactive (E)	Thorough (L)	Solve (P)	Invent (I)

The letters associated with the words you have ticked indicate your preferred style.

E   indicates an *E*nthusiastic style
I   indicates an *I*maginative style
P   indicates a *P*ractical style
L   indicates a *L*ogical style

If you are enthusiastic you tend to rush in, operate on a trial-and-error basis, adapt well to new situations and 'wear your heart on your sleeve'. People who are imaginative have a clear picture of the situation, are usually unhurried, friendly, avoid conflict and are good listeners. Practical people enjoy solving problems, tend to use facts, test out new situations and assess the results. Logical people are precise, thorough, organised and like to follow a plan. They also learn from their own experience.

Most people use all four styles at some time, but do have a preferred way of working which is usually limited to one or two styles.

Share your findings with a colleague and discuss how you might develop your non-preferred styles.

This audit is from an idea by Lacey (1999).

Step 2

Research has shown that if mentors provide their learners with lots of ideas to help them progress, the learners are more satisfied with the mentoring they receive. Are you an ideas person? If you are not, does this mean that you will not be a good mentor? All mentors have different ways of working and can be successful mentors as a result of using a range of approaches rather than one particular approach. The following 'Mentor Scale' is modified after Bell (2002). It enables you to judge your abilities in relation to the mentoring role.

The Mentor Scale

The Mentor Scale lists twenty-four sentence stems, each with two possible endings. Keeping your role as a mentor in mind, quickly review each item and circle the letter of the ending that you think best completes the sentence. **Do not leave items blank**. You may find some items in which neither ending is perfectly accurate. Select the one that seems better. After completing the Mentor Scale, score your responses using the 'Scoring Form' provided.

1.	My colleagues probably see me as	a. hard-nosed	b. a soft touch
2.	When at work the days I like most are	a. unpredictable	b. planned
3.	My colleagues generally see me as	a. formal	b. personable
4.	When it comes to social situations I	a. hold back	b. jump in
5.	Away from work activities I like to spend my time in ways that are fairly	a. spontaneous	b. routine
6.	When I encounter colleagues in need of help, I'm more likely to	a. avoid	b. get involved
7.	When I am in a team, I typically	a. follow	b. lead
8.	Most colleagues see me as	a. private	b. open
9.	When it comes to expressing my feelings, most colleagues probably see me as	a. guarded	b. comfortable
10.	When I go to a restaurant, I generally order food that	a. sounds unique	b. I know I like
11.	In general I prefer a night out to	a. the theatre	b. a party
12.	When I get angry, my emotion fuse is usually	a. short	b. long
13.	In an emergency, I would likely be	a. calm	b. anxious
14.	I am likely to be ruled by	a. logic	b. emotion
15.	When I am blamed for something I did not cause, my initial reaction is to	a. listen	b. defend
16.	Most colleagues see me as	a. an optimist	b. a pessimist
17.	Colleagues usually see me as	a. uncritical	b. critical
18.	When I work on projects, I am best at getting them	a. started	b. completed
19.	I believe that everyone should approach their work with	a. dedication	b. inspiration

continued

20. If a change is announced in my organisation I get	a. excited	b. worried
21. Colleagues are likely to see me as	a. firm	b. warm
22. After a tough day, I like to unwind	a. alone	b. with others
23. Change is most often	a. my friend	b. adversary
24. My work and social life are	a. separate	b. often overlap

The Scoring Form   'a'   'b'

Sociability
Count up your eight sociability items
1, 4, 6, 12, 14, 15, 16, 22

Totals _____ _____

Dominance
Count up your eight dominance items
2, 5, 7, 10, 13, 17, 18, 23

Totals _____ _____

Openness
Count up your eight openness items
3, 8, 9, 11, 19, 20 21, 24

Totals _____ _____

Scoring

This interpretation will help you to consider your preferred style and its potential strengths and weaknesses.

Sociability: If the 'a' score is high, you have a tendency to be not very sociable and prefer to work on your own. You must be careful to ensure that you do not appear unapproachable with your learner and may consider setting out times to speak with your learner. If the 'b' score is high then you are outgoing and should find relationship-building with your learner straightforward. However, you must beware you do not play the major role and lead in all the discussions with your learner.

Dominance: If the 'a' score is high, you are likely to allow your learner to take the lead in all developments, which you may have a problem managing. If the 'b' score is high you tend to want to be in control and take the lead in all communication. You are more likely to want to talk rather than listen.

Openness: If the 'a' score is high, you are likely to be slow to build a relationship with your learner and may even make them uncomfortable, as you are guarded in your approach. If the 'b' score is high then your relationships are more open and trusting. You tend to express your feelings easily and readily develop relationships. There is a danger that you may 'overpower' your learner with your openness.

Do you recognise yourself? Have you scored a balance between 'a' and 'b'?

Share this information with a colleague and discuss the implications of your findings.

Source: Adapted from Bell (2002)

Extended Activity 3.8

Experimenting with a coach or mentor partnership

Context

Staff development activities, however engaging, are more likely to become embedded and have impact if collaborative networking in the form of a coach or mentor relationship is available to offer support. Given that each organisation and classroom has a set of unique contextual parameters, working with a colleague who is familiar with inherent opportunities and constraints potentially increases the chances of embeddedness and impact. Will such a partnership enable the evolution of improved practice which can be sustained, and how might any improved development or performance on the part of the teacher be established?

Aims

- To establish a coach or mentor partnership for a particular purpose.
- To action and analyse a coach or mentor partnership.
- To consider the impact upon teachers involved in the partnership.
- To make suggestions concerning the possible transfer of partnerships to other contexts within the organisation.

Steps

This activity consists of four steps. Steps require that two individuals work together.

- *Step 1* involves partnership establishment.
- *Step 2* involves partnership development work and partner interaction.
- *Step 3* involves critical reflection on the personal and professional impact of the partnership and the establishment of positive and negative outcomes of the partnership.
- *Step 4* involves an analysis to consider the possible transfer of partnership to different contexts within the organisation as a whole.

Step 1

Try and answer the following questions as an aid to partnership formation.

What personal development do you hope to achieve by working in partnership?

What professional development do you hope to achieve by working in partnership?

Are there any specific aims or targets?

If so, what are they?

How do you propose to work with your partner?

- discussion?
- peer observation?
- feedback?
- to support specific learning objectives?

---

continued

- mutual problem-solving?
- a sounding-board for ideas?
- to give encouragement?

What are the personal and professional characteristics you seek in your partner?

Which individuals inside your organisation could fulfil these requirements?

Share these thoughts with your chosen individuals and establish agreement and trust with your final nominated partner. List any rules you decide upon in order that the partnership may work.

Step 2

Devise a schedule to contain mutually agreed actions each partner will undertake. For example, in the case of mutual peer-observation, a schedule compatible with timetable will need to be devised, an agreed pro forma for observation and feedback will need to be devised and an opportunity for post-observation discussion organised.

Partner 1	Partner 2
Action	Action
Action	Action
Action	Action
Action	Action
Action	Action
Action	Action

Step 3

Complete a pro forma similar to the following, in order to list both positive and negative outcomes of your own personal and professional development. Compare the completed pro forma with that of your partner.

Personal development		Professional development	
Positive	*Negative*	*Positive*	*Negative*

Step 4

Drawing on both the positive and the negative outcome of your partnership, choose another project or activity within the organisation which may benefit from a partnership approach (e.g. the introduction of a new aspect of teaching, a pupil/student behaviour issue, a weakness identified in an Ofsted report or a desire to raise performance in a particular subject of part of the teaching programme). In planning for transfer, list actions that you have found are beneficial to partnership success and actions that you have found are a hindrance to partnership success.

Suggested actions to support success	*Actions to avoid which may hinder success*

Chapter 4

Adult learning and reflective practice

What is professional learning?

The professional learning of people inside the organisation either as individuals or as part of a group contributes to organisational learning. Their collective learning potentially enables improvement across the whole organisation. According to DfES (2001f), professional learning for individuals may be considered to include elements such as:

*   having time to engage in sustained reflection;
*   participating in accredited provision through a structured programme of learning;
*   creating learning opportunities from everyday practice;
*   developing the ability to identify own learning needs;
*   developing the ability to identify the learning needs of others;
*   developing self-evaluative, observational and peer-review skills;
*   developing an individual learning plan;
*   accessing mentoring, coaching and networking;
*   assimilating professional dialogue and feedback;
*   planning longer term career aspirations.

Supporting professional learning

Engagement theory (Kearsley and Shneiderman, 1998) has emerged from teaching within electronic and distance learning environments. Despite being developed within this context, it appears to have elements of process which have resonance with the engagement of participants pursuing professional development using more traditional learning environments. Engagement theory is based upon the idea that learning activities occur in a collaborative group context, are project based and have an authentic focus. These three components are summarised by the terms *Relate*, *Create* and *Donate*. Kearsley and Shneiderman suggest:

1   *Relate*: This component emphasises team work and communication. Research on collaborative learning suggests that in the process of collaboration, participants are forced to clarify and verbalise their problems, thereby facilitating solutions. It is also suggested that collaboration increases the motivation of participants to learn. Furthermore, when participants work in teams, they often have the opportunity to work with others from different backgrounds, and this facilitates an understanding of diversity and multiple perspectives.
2   *Create*: It is suggested that this component makes learning a creative, interesting and purposeful activity. A sense of ownership and control of the project is innate, and fosters problem-based learning.
3   *Donate*: This component stresses the value of making a useful contribution while learning. The project may be work-related and fit into the team's occupational or career interests. The authentic learning context of the project potentially increases participant motivation and satisfaction.

> **Activity 4.1**
>
> **Engagement theory**
>
> Using the three principles of engagement theory – Relate, Create and Donate – take a current or future work project and draft it so as to make it potentially more engaging. Show the draft to colleagues and/or your line manager and obtain feedback. Did the promised engagement come to fruition? Did you encounter any difficulties in the feedback? How may these be overcome?

Adult learning

In exploration of coaching and mentoring, which are mechanisms to help and support learning, it is important to remember that learners who are colleagues are adults. Knowles (1980) has presented some key tenets appropriate to the understanding and engagement of adult learning:

- Adults learn best when they are involved in diagnosing, planning, implementing and evaluating their own learning.
- The role of the facilitator is to create and maintain a supportive climate that promotes the conditions necessary for learning to take place.
- Adult learners have a need to be self-directing.
- Readiness for learning increases when there is a specific need to know.
- Life's reservoir of experience is a primary learning resource and the life experiences of others add enrichment to the learning process.
- Adult learners have an inherent need for immediacy of application.
- Adults respond best to learning when they are internally motivated to learn.

Despite these useful tenets, there is continuing disagreement between the researchers on adult learning, and there is no agreed and exclusive theory for adult learning. Collarbone (2000) has identified that coaching requires the recognition that adults learn for specific purposes and they must be motivated to want to learn. Discussing the mentoring of adults, Daloz (1998) identifies potential problems that may damage intended learning relationships between colleagues. It is suggested that problems could stem from differing ethics, possible misuse of power or excessive control by the mentor, or from exaggerated emotional dependence by either party. Since learning is the fundamental process, purpose and product of coaching and mentoring (see Zachary, 2002), helping and supporting adults so as to facilitate their learning is a key skill for either the coach or the mentor. Although learning is a matter of individual interpretation of experiences, it takes place within the social context (Kerka, 1997). Therefore, the interpersonal relationship of mentor and learner is recognised as essential (Galbraith and Cohen, 1995). The idea of learning as a transaction, an interactive and evolving process between mentors and their adult learners, is considered a fundamental component of the adult mentoring relationship. The mentor is not 'the teacher' in this relationship but a more experienced and supportive colleague. Skilled mentors can bolster purposeful learning by using vision, objectives and rationale to ensure that growth has both direction (focus) and grounding (foundation) (see Bell, 2002). It is important that adult learners develop a sense of purpose to engage their enthusiasm. Rogers (1996) has summarised the research on the learning needs of adult learners and placed emphasis on the episodic nature of their learning. A mentor meets a learner regularly and is likely to provide support on specific incidents or episodes. These incidents are likely to be related to previous learning and thus would build on the experience of the learner. Other principles linked to learning in adults will also be relevant to the way in which a mentor and learner work together. Among these principles (see Table 4.1) are those suggested by Imel (1998).

Table 4.1 Implications of adult learning principles for the mentor and learner

Adult learning principles	Implications for the mentor and learner
1 Involve learners in planning and implementing learning activities.	The learner should take the lead in determining objectives and ways forward with the support and advice of the mentor.
2 Draw upon learners' experience as a resource.	The mentor should encourage, coach and nurture the learner to build on existing experience.
3 Cultivate self-direction in learners.	The mentor should help the learner to become proactive rather than reactive in teaching.
4 Create a climate that encourages and supports learning.	Meetings should be to an agenda set by the learner. The mentor should share ideas, experiences and values with the learner.
5 Foster a spirit of collaboration in the learning setting.	Both the mentor and the learner should be learning from one another. The mentor should offer support for the learner to test out new ideas.
6 Use small groups.	One-to-one is perhaps too small. The mentor could introduce the learner to other colleagues who would provide help and expertise. The learner should be encouraged to link and work with other colleagues to form their own network.

Knowledge and use of the principles of adult learning should be taken into account by a coach or mentor in determining broad strategies for working with their learner. In addition, a cognisance of the learning styles of the learner could help the coach or mentor to improve learning. FEDA (1995) proposed that: 'If teachers can understand the learning styles of individual students, they are then better equipped to anticipate their perceptions, their behaviours, their understandings and misunderstandings. Their strengths can then be built on and their weaknesses remedied or avoided.' This is reflected in FEDA's framework for learning:

The framework for learning

- Start by taking account of your learner – their experience, personal identity, their knowledge about how they learn, factors that may affect their learning.
- Define their learning objectives – by negotiation.
- Identify a strategy or strategies for achieving their objective – by agreement.
- Recognise the achievement of the objectives – this may be celebration or support.
- Review critically the learning that has taken place.
- Plan the next learning activity.

Learning styles

The way in which learners prefer to learn is indicative of their learning styles. According to Brookfield (1986), one important element in facilitating adult learning is helping learners to become aware of their own idiosyncratic learning styles. It may therefore be very worthwhile for a coach or mentor and their learner to determine their own learning styles. There are several methods that may be used for individuals to identify their learning styles.

Many of these learning inventories are based on Kolb's Learning Cycle, which proposes four modes of learning – concrete experience, reflective observation, abstract conceptualisation, and active experimentation. He determined that a learner would begin learning at any point in the cycle

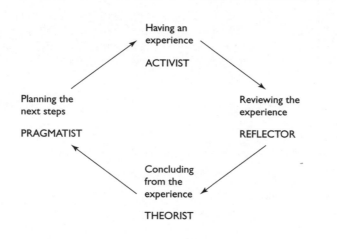

An *ACTIVIST* – will learn best by getting involved and having a go.
A *REFLECTOR* – will work on ideas and develop them with others.
A *THEORIST* – will think things through carefully and find out more.
A *PRAGMATIST* – will plan and try things out, using common sense.

Figure 4.1 The learning cycle
Source: Adapted from FEDA (1995)

and then continue around the cycle during the learning process. Honey and Mumford (1992) have adopted a learning cycle approach to indicate four stages of the learning process (see Figure 4.1).

Researchers have suggested that if the learning styles of the coach or mentor and the learner are similar, the relationship will be more successful. They will adopt the same approach to issues that arise and they do not have to reinterpret information in order to understand it. An example from Mumford (1995) illustrates this:

> If . . . we have a strong activist mentor and a strong reflector [learner] . . . the mentor may be much less willing to sit down and discuss with the [learner] what is going on, what the reasons for it are, what the facts about the situation are . . . strong activist mentors are more inclined to leap in with statements about their own experience, and to offer 'solutions', than they are carefully to review with the [learner] what the experience of the [learner] is and what it means.

Activity 4.2

Learning style

We all seem to have a learning style preference. To get the most out of learning we need to be able to use and develop our styles of learning to their maximum potential. Learners may be involved in *hearing* explanations using their ears, *seeing* text or objects using their eyes, or *doing* practical work using their bodies. The notion of learners *hearing, seeing,* or *doing* has given rise to the idea that learners may favour one of these 'styles' as a means to engage with a particular subject and then their learning can be reinforced by the adoption of other styles. The question emerges as to whether the coach or mentor and the learner do have a preferred 'style' which could be used to direct learning experiences, and to ensure that learning is engaged and supported to best effect.

Try and imagine a learning experience which has been particularly successful for you. Was there a predominance of *hearing, seeing* or *doing*?

continued

You may find that you have more than one preferred learning style. Look at the list of fifteen possible choices below. Answer either Yes or No depending on whether the proposition is one you agree with or one that you disagree with.

Proposition   Agree (Yes)   Disagree (No)

1 I learn by reading books.
2 I have trouble remembering things when I don't write
   them down.
3 I can remember pictures and diagrams in books.
4 I learn well by watching others perform.
5 I learn well by looking at text on the computer.
6 I remember things I have talked about rather than read.
7 I learn well from lectures.
8 I remember verbal instructions well.
9 I learn well from audio-tapes rather than from textbooks.
10 I like hearing the news on the radio or television rather
   than reading a newspaper.
11 I would rather perform than watch a film.
12 I am a very practical person.
13 I would rather demonstrate how to do something than
   make a speech.
14 I like it better if someone shows me what to do rather
   than just telling me.
15 I can see better how things work if I take them apart.

What does this tell you about your preferred learning style? is there any grouping in your 'Yes' responses?

Clearly 1–5 are concerned with *seeing*, 6–10 are concerned with *hearing* and 11–15 are concerned with *doing*.

Activity 4.3

Learning style and questioning

Having determined your own preferred learning style, what implication does this have for the way in which you work with your learner?

What would be the typical style of questions that you might put forward to your learner after observing them in the classroom: (1) to begin your feedback to your learner? (2) to ask your learner to explain why they carried out particular activities? (3) to ask your learner how they might improve their classroom activities?

Are these questions in a style that might be appropriate for your learner? How would you go about modifying them to meet your learner's learning style?

As the relationship between the coach or mentor and learner develops, the coach or mentor may be seen as the model of good practice. One such example of good practice is as a reflective practitioner. Irrespective of the coach or mentor's own preferred learning style and irrespective of the learner's preferred learning style, it is incumbent upon the coach or mentor, as far as possible, to encourage reflective practice on the part of the learner. Thompson (2001) has suggested that coaching without reflection will not enable learning to take place, and West-Burnham and O'Sullivan (1998) point out that both coaching and reflection are required in order to produce a consolidated and internalised learning experience.

What is reflective practice?

Good teachers are by definition reflective practitioners (see Figure 4.2), they are relentless about striving for improvement in their practice, they challenge and question themselves, they look for new and improved ways of working so that all their learners are enabled to make the best possible progress. By developing and using reflective practice you will be able to bring forward ideas to help improve and enhance your own practice, and help others to do the same.

Atkins and Murphy (1993) provide a working definition of reflective practice which should guide the coaching or mentoring process and clearly relate it to learning.

> reflection in the context of learning is a generic term for those intellectual and affective activities in which individuals engage to explore their experiences in order to lead to new understandings and appreciation.

The coach or mentor needs to support the learner in learning how to reflect. Kullman (1998) suggests that this should include the use of observation reports with mentors asking learners to think back to what happened in their lesson, usually to some specific area of their work. The mentor or coach could then use a variety of questioning techniques to lead the learner to reflect.

Reflective practice involves thinking about and learning from the learner's own practice and from the practice of others in order to gain new insights into their work so as to enable the learner to respond to new challenges in lessons as they unexpectedly arise.

Stage 1:
Identify present situation
What am I good at?
What causes concern?
What could be developed?

Stage 4:
Evaluate evidence
Has there been change?
Have I developed professionally?
Are findings contextualised in
educational literature?
How do I move forward?

Stage 2:
**How can it be changed or
improved?**
How do I go about it?
What skills do I have?
What skills do I need?

Stage 3:
Implementing and monitoring
What do I do?
What resources are available?
Who can help me?

Figure 4.2 Reflective practice

Activity 4.4

Practising your skills as a reflective practitioner

Practise your skills as a reflective practitioner by using the following framework to reflect on a professional development activity you have recently undertaken.

- Give a brief description of experience (in-house or externally provided) such as collaborating with other colleagues, observing other teachers, attendance at a training event.
- What ideas from the experience would you use in your classroom?
- What are your strengths and weaknesses with respect to implementing these ideas in your classroom?
- What sources of information could you use to help you to implement these ideas in your classroom?
- What criteria would you use to assess their positive impact in the classroom?
- How have these ideas caused you to adapt/change your professional practice?
- How would you let others in your organisation know about any successes you have achieved?
- Sources of information actually used.

Imel (1992) describes the reflective practice process of Peters (1991) which could be used as a model for supporting and developing the reflection of a learner by a mentor. The process is called DATA (see Table 4.2): **D**escribe – **A**nalyse – **T**heorise – **A**ct.

Table 4.2 Process stages of reflective practice: templates to help develop the reflective practice of your learner

Process stage of reflective practice	Reflection of the learner	Role of the mentor
Description stage	Clearly describe the issue and what the learner wishes to do about it in order to improve.	Share information based on observation.
Analytical stage	Identify those factors that contributed to the issue the learner wishes to improve. These factors may be assumptions, beliefs or rules (real or imagined).	Encourage the learner to think about their previous experience. Carry out critical questioning of the learner's assumptions.
Theorising stage	This involves the learner considering the theories that brought about the issue and to develop a new theory that would fit the required new approach.	Proposing possible theories or other people who might offer advice. Work with the learner to draw up a new theory.
Action stage	Put the new theory into action and then follow data after the results are seen.	Support the actions of the learner, reassure the learner.

Templates to help develop the reflective practice of your learner

---

Activity 4.5

Reflection on a teaching activity

Topic

- Year/Group
- What existing data has informed your work with the pupils/students?
- What does your teaching activity require pupils/students to do?
- What is the purpose of your teaching activity?
- To what extent has your activity been effective with respect to your intention? What were the strengths and weaknesses?
- What ideas/research are your tasks based on and how have they influenced you? Please quote sources of information.
- What findings did your activity result in?
- What have been the overall strengths/benefits of your teaching activity?
- What aspects do you need to improve before it is used again?
- What lessons have you learned that may be applied to your teaching overall?

Activity 4.6

Reflection on an assessment activity

Topic

- What existing data has informed your work with pupils/students?
- What does your assessment activity require pupils/students to do?
- What is the purpose of your assessment tasks?
- To what extent is it formative/summative?
- What ideas/research are your tasks based on and how have they influenced you? Please quote sources of information.
- What findings did your task result in?
- What have been the strengths/benefits of your assessment task?
- What aspects do you need to improve before it is used again?
- What lessons have you learned that may be applied to your teaching overall?

Extended activities

The remaining two 'extended' activities in this chapter are intended to further engage and challenge the reader with issues central to successful coaching, mentoring and peer-networking. Both activities are intended to capture the use of reflection so as to enhance professional learning either within or outside coaching or mentoring partnerships. The first activity sets out to further explore the use of reflective practice to increase the impact of short professional learning activities. The second activity enables the reader to engage SWOT and Force-Field analyses to facilitate reflection and enhance professional learning.

Extended activity 4.7

Increasing the impact of short professional learning activities

Context

In her book *Reflection in Learning and Professional Development*, Jennifer Moon (2002) considers the use of reflection to enhance outcomes of short courses in continuing professional development. She describes the impact of such a course as the difference the course makes to the practice of participants after they have been on the course. This impact will usually be demonstrated in improved or changed behaviour in practice. This sort of training is not always efficient in terms of whether or not participants are able to change their practice as a result of the learning. One way of making short courses more efficient in these terms is to establish that the improvement of practice is a clear learning outcome of the course. If learning outcomes are expressed in terms of change in work practice, this implies that the participants in the training need to be thinking about the implications for their work practice. A change in practice implies a conscious shift in behaviour. Simply telling people how to behave differently may be too superficial. On a short course with no time for awareness of practice to emerge gradually, Moon (2002) suggests guidance for the facilitation of reflective activities aimed at facilitating a change in practice.

Aims

- To facilitate the impact of professional learning based on short learning activities.
- To recognise change in work practice as an important learning outcome.
- To foster reflective processes through engagement with a sequence of guidance aimed at the improvement of professional practice.

Steps

This activity consists of three steps modified after Moon (2002). Steps may be undertaken by individuals working alone or in a group.

- *Step 1* involves reflection on the nature of current practice.
- *Step 2* involves reflection upon how new learning relates to current understanding.
- *Step 3* involves reflection on the nature of improved practice.

Step 1

Choose a short learning activity, one with which you are about to engage or one with which you would wish to engage. For this learning activity reflect on your current practice with respect to the content of the learning activity.

Step 2

With respect to the learning activity, reflect and clearly state what the learning activity can do to impact upon and improve your current practice. With respect to the learning activity, how will the new learning relate to what you knew or did before?

Step 3

With respect to the learning activity, how will you be able to act so that your practice is improved? What will you actually do differently?

Extended activity 4.8

Using SWOT and force-field analyses to facilitate reflection and enhance professional learning

Context

SWOT analysis aims to relate the strengths and weaknesses of an individual, team or organisation to the opportunities and threats thrown up by the changing environment in which work is carried out. Essentially, it is important to pinpoint opportunities and threats, while at the same time identifying key aspects of capability that provide strengths and weaknesses in dealing with these changing circumstances. Opportunities should be exploited and threats overcome. Force-field analysis aims to identify issues which can help us capitalise upon opportunities and move in the desired direction. This analysis also helps to identify things that are ranged against us which prevent the exploitation of opportunities and movement in the direction we seek.

Aims

- To facilitate reflection and enhance professional learning by undertaking a SWOT analysis.
- To facilitate reflection and enhance professional learning by undertaking a force-field analysis.

Steps

This activity consists of two steps. Steps may be undertaken by individuals working alone or in a group.

- *Step 1* involves performing a SWOT analysis on an event, an ongoing situation or a whole organisation.
- *Step 2* involves performing a force-field analysis on the outcomes of SWOT analysis in order to identify facilitating and resisting forces. Such forces impinge upon the realisation of opportunities and hence upon the direction we wish to take.

Step 1

With respect to an event, an ongoing situation or a direction in which you wish to move, use a SWOT analysis as a means to reflection and to act as a facilitator of your professional learning. Complete the boxes provided.

continued

Strengths	Weaknesses
Opportunities	Threats

Step 2

In identifying a desired direction in which to move, expressed in terms of opportunities to exploit, threats to overcome and current strengths and weaknesses in relation to this, a force-field analysis will allow for additional reflection and focus. Imagine your present position and the desired new position you wish to move to. There will be resisting forces which will tend to resist your movement to this new position (e.g. lack of skills or resources). There will also be pushing forces which can help you to achieve the desired new position (e.g. access to professional learning or additional funding).

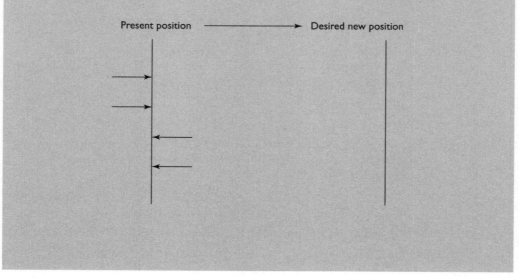

Pushing forces/Resisting forces

In order to move to your new desired position one must build up pushing forces while removing resisting forces. In the box below please list actions you could take to increase pushing forces and remove resisting forces. What actions could you take?

Actions to increase pushing forces	*Actions to remove resisting forces*

Chapter 5

The key role of the team leader
Developing skills and managing the process

Introduction

Leadership in schools and colleges within the United Kingdom has traditionally been equated with the individual such as the headteacher or college principal.

There is a growing realisation that 'dispersed' or 'delegated' leadership is crucial to institutional success (see Harris, 2002). While good teaching strongly influences learner motivation and achievement, high-quality leadership strongly influences teacher motivation and the level of teaching in classrooms (see Sergiovanni, 1999; Fullan, 2001; Muijs and Harris, 2003). The potential efficacy of approachable operational leaders who have qualities which define them as 'someone who understands the problems we are facing' rather than leadership agents within an instrumentalist and managerialist educational environment has been explored by Law (1999). A good leader secures the support, commitment and enthusiasm of staff and so enables the smooth and effective running of often complex systems of management. Leadership is about aligning people with a vision of the future and inspiring them to make it happen, even in the face of adversity. It has been suggested that leadership and management functions may be distinguished (see Rhodes, 2001) as follows:

Leadership is concerned with:

- creating and securing commitment to a clear vision;
- managing change so as to improve the school or college;
- building a high-performing team;
- inspiring, motivating and influencing staff;
- leading by example and taking responsibility.

Management is concerned with:

- strategic thinking and planning;
- people, including delegation and development;
- financial and other resources;
- communication;
- monitoring and evaluating performance and delivering results.

The emerging benefits of teacher networking and learning with and from one another within an environment of collaboration has helped to consolidate the notion of teachers as leaders.

Teacher leadership

In seeking a clear definition of teacher leadership, Muijs and Harris (2003) review the work of Katzenmeyer and Moller (2001), who see teacher leadership as having three main facets:

1   Leadership of students or other teachers: facilitator, coach, mentor, trainer, curriculum specialist, creating new approaches, leading study groups.

2 Leadership of operational tasks: keeping the school organised and moving towards its goals, through roles such as head of department, action researcher, member of task forces.
3 Leadership through decision-making or partnership: membership of school improvement teams, membership of committees; instigator of partnerships with business, higher education institutions, LEAs and parent–teacher associations.

Day and Harris (2003) suggest four dimensions to teacher leadership with respect to organisational improvement:

1 Translating the principles of school improvement into practices within classrooms.
2 Fostering a collaborative way of working so as to engage the participation and ownership of other teachers with respect to developments and changes.
3 Mediating through their expertise, information and access to other resources.
4 Forging relationships with other teachers so that mutual learning takes place.

It is evident that teacher leadership is both skilful and demanding. Expression of teacher leadership within the context of team leadership entails a combination of concern for people with an ability to get things done. This is reflected by Fleming (2000), who suggests that the following five factors are implicit in people working together as a team:

1 vision and sense of direction;
2 the behaviour of the team leader;
3 the extent to which people pull together;
4 open lines of communication;
5 regular reviews of progress.

Not all groups of people working together may be identified as a team.

Groupings and team work

Within professional contexts, Downey (2001) suggests that a number of different groupings of people may be identified:

- *A work community*: A group of people who occupy the same work space but whose tasks are probably not shared. Individuals pursue their own jobs and are not dependent on each other for their success. The need for a high level of relationship is low.
- *A working group*: A group of people who have a shared task, such as a committee or working party. They are dependent on each other for the success of the task but not for their overall success. The need for a high level of relationship is medium.
- *A team*: A group of people who have shared goals and a common purpose for which they are collectively and mutually accountable. The need for a high level of relationship is very high.

Activity 5.1

What is your own management orientation?

Critically reflect on your own management orientation. Are you people-orientated or task-orientated? Place yourself within one of the boxes A–D (modified after Fleming (2000)). Then identify your management style using the descriptions provided below.

continued

	Low task-orientated	High task-orientated
High people-orientated	A	D
Low people-orientated	C	B

What are your strengths and weaknesses with respect to actual or intended team leadership?

Box A managers: *People managers*

Trust team members to get on with their jobs. Being considerate to all, there is a danger that people managers may fail to give a clear sense of direction to the team. They may also fail to develop the potential of those in their team.

Box B managers: *Authoritarian managers*

Are efficient and well organised with a clear sense of actions required to move their team forward. Authoritarian managers may fail to adequately involve colleagues in decision-making and goal-setting. They may fail to develop team members to perform to the best of their ability.

Box C managers: Laissez-faire *managers*

Are weak on both task and people skills. They may fail to manage and tasks may not get done. Team members may be left completely alone with no direction or support.

Box D managers: *Omega managers*

Are able to accomplish tasks coupled with concern for team members. They offer direction and are supportive to team members. Being good listeners, they are able to engage team members' skills.

Team leadership and developing others

In addition to creating and maintaining effective working relationships within the team and between the team and other colleagues, team leaders have an important role in developing and supporting the team and the individuals within it. Team leaders need to be skilled as coaches, mentors and networkers so as to enhance the performance of the team and support the development of the members within it. The professional growth of staff can depend very much upon the team leader's ability to encourage and enable teachers' professional learning.

However, Thompson (2001) reports that in a survey of teachers in schools following threshold assessment, one-third of respondents did not agree that their team leader was good at coaching and developing them; and one-fifth said that the team leader did not take a close interest in their professional development. The survey also pointed to the fact that teachers who were confident of passing the threshold were twice as likely to regard their managers as good at coaching and developing them, and more likely to trust their managers and feel they took a close concern in their professional development. Training for team leaders in the interpersonal and professional skills of coaching and mentoring presents a high priority.

Coaching for successful team performance

Coaching involves helping other people to develop their skills and knowledge. Parsloe and Wray (2000) suggest that potential – interference = performance. They also suggest, therefore, that the main role of a coach is to reduce or remove the 'interferences' which prevent an individual or team from producing their optimum levels of performance. In a team coaching session, Downey (2001) suggests the use of the GROW or To GROW method:

To   Topic for the session
G   Goal for the session
R   Reality of the contextual issues surrounding the topic
O   Options for a way forward with the topic
W   Wrap up the session with agreement about the next steps.

Activity 5.2

Critically analyse your skills as a team coach

Prepare to employ the To GROW method in your next team meeting.

How different is this from your usual system?

Which steps do you feel most comfortable/uncomfortable with?

Use the To GROW method in your next team meeting

- Was the method successful for you?
- What were the strengths/weaknesses?
- What would you do differently next time?

Sometimes team members may ask the team leader acting in the role of coach for help when the team leader is busy pursuing other tasks. Such pleas for help, if not answered, may eventually jeopardise the coach/learner relationship. Given that team leaders are under increasing pressure, the question emerges as to how quickly they can meet the needs of team members. Parsloe and Wray (2000) suggest that the use of a 3-D technique can be effective in these circumstances. This technique enables the coach to quickly define the problem and empower the team member to pursue possible solutions. The problem is explored in terms of the situation (e.g. lack of resources), the people involved (e.g. students or pupils) and the team members themselves (e.g. lack of knowledge), hence the term 3-D technique.

The qualities required by the team leader acting as a coach to individuals or as a team coach reflect their good interpersonal skills, their willingness to manage difficult staff and their ability to engage team members in the leadership process.

Activity 5.3

A technique for responding quickly to team member requests for help

In order to respond more rapidly to team members' request for help, consider the use of the following 3-D technique. Assess the effectiveness of helping team members to help themselves.

1   Ask the team member to define the problem clearly and simply.
2   How does the problem relate to:
  • the situation:
  • the people involved?
  • the learner?
3   Identify the priority issue(s).
4   Generate and choose one or more options to make progress.
5   Ask the team member to pursue the agreed action.

Source: Modified after Parsloe and Wray (2000)

Developing qualities and skills relevant to coaching and raising performance within the team

Activity 5.4

Developing your questioning technique

Coaches and mentors need to use questioning effectively in order to establish development issues and to encourage reflection on the part of their learners. Not all types of questions are useful for these purposes. For example, closed questions inviting a 'yes' or 'no' answer, leading questions framed to expect certain responses or multiple questions which can be confusing, may all serve to limit constructive dialogue.

Develop your questioning using the examples below:

Open questions can stimulate discussion

e.g. What do you think is the best way forward?
Decide on a series of open questions of your own and write them in the space provided:

Try them out with the help of a colleague

  • What feedback did you receive?
  • Was your questioning technique well received by your colleague?
  • What strengths and weaknesses were perceived?

Reflective questions allow for confirmation of understanding and an opportunity to think more deeply about issues e.g. Can I check with you what you are proposing to do to overcome that particular problem? Decide on a series of reflective questions of your own and write them in the space provided:

Try them out with the help of a colleague

- What feedback did you receive?
- Was your questioning technique well received by your colleague?
- What strengths and weaknesses were perceived?

Activity 5.5

Dealing with conflict

The team leader acting as a coach is placed in a position of seeking to enable team members and the team as a whole to develop and perform well. The management of interpersonal relationships is complex. The team leaders' skills will be tested to the full when responding to and attempting to engage staff presenting barriers to team involvement and learning.

Recall a recent instance of conflict or a possible future instance of conflict with a colleague or team member. This may be located in any area of working (e.g. unwillingness to contribute to meetings, resistance to change or refusal to accept a team decision).

Having identified your area of conflict or potential conflict, formulate possible response(s). Use the following possible responses as examples for your guidance:

Response 1:   Seek them to reflect on the issue and ask them what they would do to overcome difficulties?

Response 2:   Let them know that you are upset and say that you will offer them some extra help.

Response 3:   Arrange a formal meeting and tell them what is expected and that you will monitor their actions closely.

Your preferred response(s):

Discuss your instance of conflict and preferred response with an experienced colleague whom you trust. Do they support your response given the circumstances? What alternative strategies can they suggest?

Activity 5.6

Sharing leadership

Engaging team members in the leadership process offers potential professional growth to the team, and encourages and enables individual members' professional learning. Team leaders in the role of coach seeking such team empowerment entail the conveyance to members that leadership is an activity in which they all have a share.

Hold discussions with each team member and try to establish:

1   Their perceptions of team leadership listing areas of agreement and areas of disagreement with your own perceptions.
2   Their perceptions of their opportunities to share in team leadership.
3   How they feel they may be empowered to share in team leadership.

*   What areas for development have you uncovered?
*   How can action be taken to address such developments?
*   What do you perceive as the benefits/disadvantages of empowering team members?

Extended activities

The remaining two 'extended' activities in this chapter are intended to further engage and challenge the reader with issues central to successful coaching, mentoring and peer-networking. The first activity sets out to explore support for poorly performing teachers within the team. The second activity enables the reader to further explore how resolution of problems encountered by the team may be addressed.

Extended activity 5.7

An analysis of the causes of poor teacher performance within the team

Context

The emotional, psychological and financial investment made by those involved in addressing poor performance is high. It is incumbent upon leaders and managers to act sensitively and professionally in understanding the causes of poor performance, and thus offer an intervention appropriate to securing the most positive and beneficial outcomes for all concerned, including pupils and students. Although it is unlikely that individual teachers will perform poorly in all aspects of their work, the construction of poor performance may engage some or all of the following sources of evidence:

*   performance criteria;
*   complaints from parents;
*   complaints from pupils or students;
*   complaints from other teaching colleagues;
*   the disruptive behaviour of pupils or students;
*   senior manager informal monitoring;
*   monitoring of other leaders and managers;

- feedback from inspectors;
- poor examination results.

Support to remediate poor performance may take a variety of forms and may include coaching, mentoring, other professional development activities and/or work reorganisation. An accurate identification of the causes underlying poor teacher performance would assist in informing the nature of any intervention. The background to poor teacher performance may be quite complex; for example, Fidler and Atton (1999) identify the causes of poor performance as rooted in either management, the job or the individual, and claim that attempts to deal with poor performance should look at each of these three causes in order.

Aims

- To undertake an analysis of possible causes of poor teacher performance within your own team/organisation.
- To present this analysis as a means to facilitate dialogue between individuals either as part of remediation of actual poor performance or as a means to enhance understanding, collaboration and cooperation.

Steps

This activity consists of two steps. The first step may be undertaken by someone working alone. Group work throughout is preferable.

- *Step 1* involves completion of a table to facilitate dialogue concerning the possible causes of poor teacher performance within the team/organisation.
- *Step 2* involves presentation of findings and the initiation of dialogue within the team/organisation.

Step 1

The following table has been modified after Rhodes and Beneicke (2003). Complete the table in order to effect an analysis of the possible causes of poor teacher performance within the team/organisation.

Possible cause of poor performance	Organisational problems	Management problems	Team problems	Post-related problems	Personal problems
Organisational structure					
Organisational systems					
The job role					
Professional development support					
Resource availability					
Leadership					

continued

Step 2

Following completion of the table and analysis, summarise findings so that a sympathetic dialogue may be undertaken either as part of remediation of actual poor performance or as a means to enhance understanding, collaboration and cooperation between individuals. Plan for dialogue, as this will involve feedback and possibly constructive criticism. If done well it can encourage development; if done badly it can damage relationships. The following headings may help in your planning.

Try and add notes to your findings using the headings as guidance.

Feedback (avoid judgementalism, encourage dialogue)

- positive aspects:
- specific comments to aid personal learning:
- items which can be changed:
- change strategies which could be considered:

Criticism (avoid causing resentment, be constructive)

- specific issue(s) with examples:
- offer discussion:
- possible solutions emerging from discussion:
- the accepted solution:
- support needed to effect the agreed solution:
- agreed issue(s) review protocol:

Extended activity 5.8

Fostering a collaborative team environment for problem resolution

Context

The team leaders seeking to foster team collaboration are actively supporting the team to:

- promote the sharing of experience;
- promote open communication;
- promote the sharing of problems, generating alternative solutions, and selecting appropriate and feasible alternatives;
- provide assistance and encouragement;
- provide for a supportive work environment so that all team members can feel they are achieving professional growth and learning;
- foster an environment in which coaching and mentoring can flourish.

Aims

- To foster team collaboration by sharing the resolution of a problem encountered by the team with the team itself.
- To prepare and implement a plan to overcome the problem which has been formulated and agreed by the whole team.

Steps

This activity consists of three steps. Steps should be undertaken by engaging the whole team.

- *Step 1* involves seeking information about the problem encountered by the team so as to arrive at a joint definition of the problem.
- *Step 2* involves the joint evolution of strategies to overcome the problem.
- *Step 3* involves the formulation of an implementation plan.

Step 1

As a team, seek information about the problem in question and define the problem.

Step 2

As a team, propose alternative strategies and select the strategies that will actually be implemented.

Step 3

Design an implementation plan.

Objective(s):

Actions to be undertaken and by whom:

Success criteria:

Resources:

Target date for achievement:

Review date:

Chapter 6

Leadership coaching
Developing the profession by collaboration

From competition to collaboration

The principle of encouraging the development of collaboration within schools and colleges in a planned or systematic way is part of the increasing focus upon the perceived need for leadership management and training at all levels. Perversely this is occurring against the backdrop of the legacy of autonomy and competition between different institutions, which was previously encouraged as a key component of the raising standards debate. The fact that schools and colleges will face similar challenges and will have to respond to common initiatives was seemingly disregarded in the belief that encouraging competitiveness with achievements measured by league table performance was the means by which standards would be raised. The debate has moved on from an absolute focus upon the key role of the headteacher in engendering school improvement, and has broadened to encompass the contribution of others. Over time the inescapable realisation that the performance of the organisation comprises the contributions of the individuals within it takes us some way towards realising why the rhetoric has moved beyond training school and college leaders in isolation, to the broader needs of all those within the organisation. While the training needs of the senior teams, and in particular the headteachers and principals, are still to the fore, the debate has moved towards the principles of 'distributed leadership' (see Gronn, 2000) and its potential to impact upon, and more particularly to sustain, change. Recent research within the school context has confirmed that equipping classroom teachers to lead innovation and development can sustain improvement and capacity-building (Harris and Chapman, 2002).

Current moves towards a focus upon workforce reform are intended to both reinforce the key role of the teacher and to provide some reprioritisation of activities and tasks to liberate teaching time and give a clearer focus upon classroom activity. While teachers need to be acknowledged for their talents, skills and abilities, they must also be allowed and encouraged to share these valuable assets with colleagues. This need has been heightened by the growth of support staffing within the education sector, where classroom assistants and learning mentors form part of the overall staffing portfolio. Initially, teachers in schools and colleges may be reluctant to collaborate and share, particularly beyond the boundaries of their own organisation, but McCann and Radford (1993) indicated that teachers involved in collaboration with their colleagues reported considerable personal benefits from this collaborative activity. This study also suggested that teachers felt that collaboration improved their communication skills, gave them a sharper work-related focus, increased the amount of time they spent reflecting upon their work, and enhanced their self-esteem and confidence in their teaching ability.

Collaborative working appears to be strongest where there is reciprocal learning, and consequently the benefits are apparent to all concerned. In their study McCann and Radford identify three characteristics needed for successful collaborative work:

- *Educational leadership*: Leadership teams must support and encourage collaboration in order to foster a positive learning environment for teachers:

    Educational leaders should share with teachers a disciplined curiosity about teaching and join with them in mastering and advancing this complex human activity.

- *Time*: Organisations should not expect there to be a correlation between the quantity and the quality of work. The focus should be upon improving the quality of teaching to enhance the prospect of reciprocal learning.
- *Motivation*: Staff need to be highly motivated and prepared if they are to meet the intellectual and emotional demands of collaborative working:

> Teachers are motivated to participate with one another to the degree that they require each other's contributions in order to succeed in their own work.

Thus collaborative working has to be seen as part of the culture and ethos of the school or college, and the greatest impact across the organisation will be felt if this is the case. Clearly, individual pockets of good practice can still exist; where this does occur, these are often based upon personal friendships or good working relationships within an individual department or section. However, before moving on to a consideration of the principles and techniques of leadership coaching, it is important to remember that for this to have maximum impact a basis of collaborative working is an essential prerequisite.

Leadership training and development

In a study of leadership in schools, Southworth (2002) reported that when asked, headteachers said that they had learned most and developed their leadership and management practices by doing the job. Such 'learning on the job' requires heads who are engaged in continuous professional learning problem-solving through reflection on the challenges they meet in the course of their everyday work. Importantly, if effective professional development for leadership is characterised by 'on the job' learning, then training for leaders using content-driven courses aimed at developing new knowledge may be less effective than the engagement of group or one-to-one activities in which leaders share and develop key ideas and insights from their work within their own professional context.

In an evaluation of the UK National Professional Qualification for Headship (NPQH), Ofsted (2002) suggested that the school-based aspects of the training were the least effective parts of the programme. It was reported that some candidates even had difficulty undertaking a school-based project because their school was not supportive and was not able to provide opportunities for them to experience leadership. The importance of substantial contextualised organisation-based experiences in fostering leadership development concomitant with the potential to build change capacity has already received much attention. For example, in describing leadership within a culture of change, Fullan (2001) makes the point that 'organisations transform when they can establish mechanisms for learning in the dailiness of organisational life'.

According to Elmore (2000), fundamental transitions happen when people have:

> many opportunities to be exposed to ideas, to argue them to their own normative belief systems, to practice the behaviours that go with those values, to observe others practicing those behaviours, and, most importantly, to be successful at practicing in the presence of others.

It is hard to see how the very best off-site training, even with the most realistic of simulations and periodic school-based elements, could provide this sort of daily experience. Very good external training could even be counter-productive in that it could result in enthusiastic new leaders returning to school unable to put into practice what they have learned and therefore reinforcing the view that transformation is unrealistic. The possible benefits of in-house coaching or mentoring of leaders and potential leaders thus emerges.

The notion of dispersed or distributed leadership is beginning to emerge in colleges. Lumby (2003) reports that much of government policy in relation to both the school and the college sectors has conceptualised leadership as something that an individual, notably the principal, does. Lumby argues that leadership is not the same as management delegation or culture or vision, but it

Activity 6.1

The distribution of leadership?

Although the following research is school-based, distributed leadership, or lack of it, has resonance in colleges within the further education sector.

Hopkins and Jackson (2002) remind us just how challenging the distribution of leadership can be:

> Schools are not currently well designed for either capacity creation or distributed leadership building. Some are weak in the foundation conditions, turbulent, under strain, riven by conflicting pressures. Others are rendered incoherent by the forces of external change, the reform agenda and the expectations of multiple accountabilities. Some schools are inarticulate about shared values, unclear about the beliefs that unite them. Most (secondary in particular) have structures designed when stability and the management of stasis were the expectations.

Muijs and Harris (2003) report on studies which illustrate how school leaders provide opportunities to participate in decision-making and lead in school development. The following possibilities are included:

- sharing decision-making power with staff;
- allowing staff to manage their own decision-making committees;
- taking staff opinion into account;
- providing autonomy for teachers;
- altering working conditions so that staff have collaborative planning time;
- ensuring adequate involvement in decision-making related to new initiatives in the school;
- creating opportunities for staff development.

What prominence does each of these facets have within your own professional context?

On a scale of 1 (low) to 10 (high), do you feel the organisation is prepared for distributed leadership?

Make a list of the barriers to distributed leadership within your organisation. Think of one way in which you might contribute to the preparation of your organisation for distributed leadership.

subsumes and is created through all three. It is not the gift of an individual but is created by the community, and as such offers the opportunity for many to contribute.

In an article concerned with perspectives on leadership and school improvement, Jackson (2000) provided the following hypothesis to stimulate reflection on leadership action for organisational improvement:

> In actively improving schools, the focus will tend to be less upon the characteristics of 'the leader' than upon creating shared contexts for adult learning about leadership. School leaders in these schools will develop leadership capacity. They will 'give away' leadership and coach others to be successful. Leadership for school improvement operates significantly in the domains of induction and coaching, cultural transmission and values articulation and it is a widely shared function.

Activity 6.2

Leadership training in your own organisation

Reflect upon preparation for leadership roles within your own organisation. Here are four benchmarks for leadership training:

1   Preparation for leadership is not a feature of professional development within the organisation.
2   Preparation for leadership entails attendance at externally provided courses.
3   Preparation for leadership is informal and emerges from involvement with projects inside the organisation.
4   Preparation for leadership is more formal and emerges from involvement with projects inside the organisation supported by a coach or a mentor.

Where would you place your organisation with respect to these benchmarks? What opportunities can you identify within your own organisation to initiate the development of leaders so that leadership may become more distributed?

Widening our understanding of the contexts in which leadership learning occurs may provide a framework for greater organisational and individual leadership learning capability. For example, the development of emotional intelligence has been associated with the ability to succeed in management and leadership roles.

Clutterbuck and Megginson (1999) suggest that mentors can help build greater understanding and strengths in five areas of emotional intelligence:

1   knowing one's own emotions;
2   managing emotions;
3   motivating yourself;
4   recognising emotions in others;
5   managing relationships with others.

Activity 6.3

Exploring emotional intelligence: knowing and managing one's own emotions

With a partner try and separate the emotional and intellectual content of a selected issue.

*   What was the issue?
*   Did your feelings change as a result of the issue?
*   Do you usually feel a particular way as a result of issues of this kind?

Develop greater control of emotions. With the same partner and the same issue explore your management of emotions.

*   Is the way you feel appropriate?
*   How do you think you should feel?
*   How can you use your emotions to achieve goals?

Activity 6.4

Exploring emotional intelligence: managing relationships with others

With a partner explore the following:

- In a leadership/conflict situation which you have to resolve, how do you want the recipients of your intervention to feel?
- How will you manage your own emotions?
- How do you motivate others?
- How do you influence people to your way of thinking?

Activity 6.5

Critical incident analysis

This analysis can help you to revisit previous learning experiences and to reflect and realise what you have learned. It is also a mechanism to probe assumptions that have informed your understanding or action with respect to the incident.

   With a partner, independently write a full description of an incident which has had an impact on both of you. Read out your descriptions to each other and try to identify differences in perspective.

- What did you learn from the incident?
- What assumptions influenced your understanding or action?
- What might you do differently next time?
- Why?

Mentoring vs. coaching

As the principles of leadership and management within the context of schools and colleges have developed, many of the same assumptions held widely in private sector management circles have been embraced. Consequently, the suggestion that experienced managers should offer support as a regular part of the professional development available to aspiring managers is now accepted and forms part of current senior leadership training. Mentoring and coaching have become an integral part of the professional development vocabulary, but are at their most effective when the climate for collaborative working has been established (as described above). Torrance (1984, quoted in Hansford *et al.*, 2002) suggests that organisations which contain 'individuals who remained mentor-less were more vulnerable to a range of problems such as educational failure, lack of career goals and focus, lack of enthusiasm, frustrated creativity and unfulfilling jobs'. Given that the opposite is also said to be true, it would appear that we are closer to understanding the holy grail of educational improvement if all these potential problems can be overcome by mentoring. However, before rushing headlong towards mass implementation it would be as well to consider the findings of Scandura *et al.* (1996), who considered that 'each mentor's world is unique, shaped by personal, professional and other situational motives'. Consequently a carefully considered, contextualised and bespoke model is required, and once again we find that there is no short cut to success.

   This careful contextualisation of the use of mentoring is crucial, for, as with many other strands of professional development activity, there is no off-the-shelf package to be taken and applied generically. As Gibb (1994) pointed out: 'providing a conceptual framework for understanding and analysing the diversity of mentoring in modern organisations is – a major issue facing those concerned with the effective development and evaluation of organised mentoring of formal schemes.'

Elsewhere in this book the differences between coaching and mentoring have been explored; coaching, which is the principal focus of this chapter, is seen as being related to mentoring but it is a discrete activity. Phillips (1995) stated that coaching has 'clear and unique advantages and [consequently it] is establishing itself alongside related activities, such as mentoring . . . as a key development technique'. As has already been said, for coaching to succeed the overall ethos and 'climate' within the school or college have to be conducive to its implementation. As with so many other initiatives, good schools and colleges will have been adopting the principles of coaching long before it became part of the current vocabulary of management training. The best coaches are skilled facilitators content to observe while still being available to give guidance and help when required. The learning from the process takes place within the context of the workplace, and although the learning points can be quite specific, it is important that their application is perceived as being generic. Thus the argument, which can be proposed by both individuals and organisations that the learning from coaching is totally situation-specific, can be refuted.

A more hierarchical definition of this activity is provided by Kilburg (1996, as defined in Rider, 2002, p.233):

> Coaching is defined as a helping relationship between a client (who has managerial authority and responsibility) and a coach who uses a wide variety of behavioural techniques and methods to help the client achieve a mutually identified set of goals to improve his or her professional performance and personal satisfaction and consequently to improve the effectiveness of the client's organisation within a formally defined coaching agreement.

Kilburg's definition suggests a context for coaching which places it within the domain of what has become accepted as 'executive coaching'. This activity normally relies upon the coach being an outside expert with an emphasis upon leadership development. Most of the current rhetoric from both the National College for School Leadership and the current offerings within FE leadership training suggest this model. However, there is an emerging bank of research which suggests that while this may be the starting point for the introduction and formalisation of this activity, that ultimately it will permeate throughout the organisation and may be performed by anyone at any level (see Bowerman and Collins, 1999).

Ultimately, coaching is concerned with creating the conditions which will help people perform to the best of their ability. Consequently it has a clear and direct link to the best principles of management development and touches at the heart of quality-related issues. As Phillips indicated,

> a learner who is being coached will feel a sense of ownership and that they are managing their own development. It is a short step from managing your own learning to managing your own performance, a cornerstone of concepts such as empowerment and performance management.

This view was supported by Redshaw (2000), who argued that coaching

> systematically increases the capability and work performance of someone by exposing him or her to work-based tasks or experiences that will provide the relevant learning opportunities, and give guidance and feedback to help him or her to learn from them.

Coaching within a collaborative environment as described earlier in this chapter can be a professionally fulfilling and empowering experience. It will strengthen the organisation and play a major part in the professional development and personal fulfilment of the participating staff; both those providing the coaching and those who are the learners, or recipients. However, the skills of the coach do not sit easily with some of the traditional perceptions of leadership and management, and leaders who are competitive and like to be in control of tightly focused agendas are unlikely themselves to be enabling coaches, or contribute to a climate where such techniques will flourish. Consequently if we are to address the central theme of this chapter and develop the profession by collaboration, we may need to re-examine some of our traditional views of leadership and management styles, strategies and training. New models are being developed which take us beyond the traditional models of the training and recruitment of headteachers and other senior managers and begin to explore the benefits of leadership coaching.

Leadership coaching in practice

The Midlands Leadership Centre (MLC) is based within the University of Wolverhampton and is directed by the Dean of Education. The MLC has sought to take a proactive role in the improvement of educational standards in the schools and colleges of the Black Country region in which it is based. Being an urban area, the Black Country is more densely populated than the average nationally and has a higher proportion of families from ethnic minority backgrounds than elsewhere in the West Midlands. When compared nationally, the area has clear patterns of concentrated deprivation. Four local education authorities oversee compulsory education in the Black Country, with the local Learning and Skills Council having responsibility for post-16 education. Although the numbers of young people attaining more educationally are increasing, a significant minority of young people are under-performing in comparison to West Midlands and national averages. Several schools within the Black Country have received adverse Ofsted inspections and more recently some of the FE college provision has also received some unfavourable inspection comment. Even more fundamentally, three of the four local education authorities have also been deemed to be 'failing' as a result of their external inspection processes.

The MLC on behalf of the DfES has conceived the idea of a Black Country School Improvement Partnership, which seeks to provide a range of quality-assured services to schools through a collaborative partnership between the four LEAs, the University and private sector partners. As part of this, issues concerning the recruitment and retention of staff have required new and potentially radical solutions. Within the local education authority with the most serious issues of deprivation and underachievement, the recruitment of staff to headteacher posts is extremely problematic. Where the schools concerned have received adverse Ofsted inspections, the problems are compounded. Difficulties with school budgets also eliminate the strategy, which has been tried elsewhere, of paying inflated salaries in a bid to attract appropriate applicants. Neighbouring boroughs are also experiencing recruitment difficulties and this fact, together with historically poor perceptions of the borough with the most difficulties, made recruitment of teachers, and in particular senior managers, highly problematic.

Following discussions between senior personnel from the local education authority and the MLC the concept of professional secondments offered via the University with coaching support from the MLC was initiated. The concept was to offer full or partial secondments for either aspirant headteachers or for existing heads who would welcome the opportunity to share their expertise in a different context. Opportunities for research, with the possibility of gaining accreditation, were also part of the package. The coaching support provided by the MLC was seen as a key element for reasons outlined by Rider (2002): 'coaching is valued for its capacity to enable managers and executives to learn and develop, and thereby to enhance their personal and organisational effectiveness.' The process was conceived as a 'win-win' with benefits accruing on all sides; as Rider once again suggests, the aim was 'for organisations to frame coaching in terms of individual development with organisational benefits'. Collaboration with neighbouring local education authorities was crucial to enable the release of appropriate staffing and to deal with the personnel requirements associated with the secondments. Fortunately, the Black Country School Improvement Partnership had helped to create and establish the ground rules for this collaboration. Two case studies will be featured below as practical examples of 'Leadership coaching; developing the profession by collaboration'.

Activity 6.6

A third party in leadership coaching?

To what extent do you perceive the role of a third party – in this case the University – as crucial in facilitating the process and subsequent coaching?

What do you see as the benefits to existing experienced headteachers in participating in this process?

Case study A

School A had been identified as a school facing difficulties and had therefore attracted 'Intervention Funding' from the DfES. Leadership and management within the school had been identified as a key issue; one indicator of this was the extremely large budget deficit. External examination results were poor and the application of value-added data indicated that the school was dramatically under-performing. The community had lost confidence in their school, with local parents opting to send their children across the border for secondary education. The substantive headteacher had departed suddenly, and an acting headteacher who had been recruited from a private sector agency had been in post for almost a year. Previous attempts to recruit a substantive headteacher had proved unsuccessful and there was a real sense of crisis regarding the school's future.

The recruitment process for those interested in the secondment opportunities described in the previous section had generated a number of possibilities for this school. Given the particular circumstances, it was decided that a period of stability was crucial and, that as there was no substantive leader to coach or support, the preferred solution was to place an aspirant headteacher, seconded from their school for a prolonged period. In addition to the support provided through the MLC it was decided to place an additional, existing, appropriately experienced headteacher alongside the full-time secondee for two days per week. The acting 'step-in' headteacher would be phased out, but this would occur over a short period of time, so that it would not further destabilise the school. There was much discussion over titles, which would obviously be instrumental in shaping the perceptions of the key stakeholders, namely pupils and parents. It was decided that the experienced, partially seconded head would be known as the 'Executive Headteacher' and that the full-time secondee would be known as the 'Associate Headteacher'. Initially, both of these individuals would be operating alongside the Acting Headteacher and, in spite of the best endeavours of all concerned, there was inevitably some initial confusion. Year eleven students were about to witness their fifth headteacher and, not surprisingly, some of their first comments to the Associate Headteacher were:

'Are you going to stay?'
'How long are you going to stay?'
'Who is the actual Headteacher?'

Several parts of the plan were implemented quickly for, while this confusion and uncertainty may have been predictable, for the model to succeed it could not be allowed to continue for any length of time. The Acting Headteacher left quite quickly after the new arrangements were put into place. For the Associate Headteacher, who was known to be interested in a promotion to the position of Headteacher, this represented an excellent professional development opportunity. Substantively she was a deputy headteacher in a neighbouring authority, and a key part of the MLC's role was to negotiate her secondment from this post for a two-year period. This was assisted by the fact that her headteacher was resigned to her going, recognising that she had previously come close to being appointed elsewhere. The merits of the professional development opportunity on offer helped to secure the necessary release. The opportunities presented by this long-term secondment for internal professional development opportunities within the donor school were also an attractive prospect.

The Executive Headteacher had been in his post for a number of years, leading a successful school. His partial secondment represented an opportunity for him to use his skills within a different context as well as giving a clear acknowledgement of his achievements as a headteacher. Later in the process when a review of titles and roles was muted, it was suggested that he become more of a critical friend; while a shift in modes of operation was possible, he was keen to retain the title of executive headteacher alongside his responsibility for the school budget.

The concept of freeing the Associate Headteacher of financial management – she shadowed the Executive Headteacher in this role – allowed her to assume day-to-day responsibility for running the school. Throughout this initial period of assuming responsibility for what was by any definition a challenging school, she was supported and coached by the Executive Headteacher and initially also by the Acting Headteacher:

> 'The opportunity to work alongside two experienced headteachers provided an initial comfort zone. I was able to shadow and effectively learn on the job. I observed practice confirming my ideas about leadership, I also very quickly learnt how not to do things – I was given the task of strategic development and shadowed at budget meetings – the departure of the Acting Headteacher gave me the opportunity to take the responsibility I was ready to assume. The first term in post proved to be an exceptional learning experience.'

As well as providing support within the school the MLC was also engaged with governors and the local education authority to provide feedback and to assist with the strategic planning concerning the school's future. The initial monitoring and feedback were extremely positive and, given the relative stability of the school, governors were confident that they could progress to the appointment of a substantive headteacher, something that had previously proved difficult to achieve. The two-year secondment had initially been negotiated in order that this process need not be rushed, and there was certainly a view that this process could have been deferred for a little longer. The governors decided that twelve months after the secondment process commenced they would like a substantive headteacher in post and the position was advertised during the spring term. After two days of competitive interviews the Associate Headteacher was appointed. The governors were delighted that they had secured someone of her calibre; similarly the local education authority had secured an external candidate whom they had had the chance to evaluate over an extended period of time 'in situ'.

There are clearly a number of learning points which emerge from this model in terms of the theme of 'Leadership coaching: developing the profession by collaboration'. The role of the detached third party is a crucial one; in this case the MLC brokered the dialogue between local education authorities and schools. All schools need to seek to nurture good leaders and managers, and while this may be understood, it is often for internal benefit within the school or local education authority. For schools and local education authorities to release their brightest stars in situations other than that of direct appointment, a broader view of professional development and collaboration has to exist. For the secondee, coaching and support are crucial, and while there may be some basic principles which can be applied, the precise details of the nature of these support structures will vary depending upon the circumstances of particular schools. Nor is this a precise science; in the mind of the secondee described above, speaking in her new role as substantive headteacher and reflecting upon her experience, she feels that: 'It is acceptable to receive coaching/ advice upon the school budget but the coach should not take control of it. By doing so, the learner has limited opportunity to develop the necessary budgetary skills.' This comment lies at the heart of the subtlety of performing the coach's role as alluded to above. It is perhaps also appropriate that this case study should conclude with a final reflection from the newly appointed head.

> 'Having successfully completed NPQH, neither this nor any other qualification, while useful from a theoretical perspective, offers little practical experience for future headship. Anyone

aspiring to headship should have the opportunity to gain real, hands-on experience of running a school. The opportunity I had to take up Associate Headship via the MLC has proved to be perhaps the most valuable experience of my career.'

Case study B

This study is concerned with the application of the same model within another secondary school in the same local education authority. On this occasion the school had been formally placed in the Ofsted category of requiring 'special measures'; or in common parlance it was a 'failing' school. Previously it had been among the highest performing schools in the borough, achieving consistently high examination results. The quality of leadership and management was a key issue within the school's failure. The school was felt by its local education authority to have worked within a comfort zone generated by its historic examination results, using traditional systems which had been effective in previous years. Changes to the school's intake in relation to ethnicity and behaviour had created new problems that had not been addressed. The school's historical success in terms of league table performance had also created over-subscription, which meant temporary classrooms and additional wear and tear upon existing buildings. Any extra finance which had accrued from the additional pupil numbers did not appear to have been invested in the buildings. Apart from the key issue of the deficiencies in strategic leadership and management, the other key findings from Ofsted were:

- teaching and learning – specific departments and general quality;
- pupil behaviour;
- communication with parents/local community;
- health and safety – a plethora of issues about practice, policy and the quality of buildings.

In liaison with the school governors, the local education authority agreed that the headteacher should stand down. No other staffing changes were made. The agreed model with the MLC was to place an Associate Headteacher paired for two days a week with an existing local head (Executive Headteacher).

Although similar to the previous case study on this occasion there was no existing or acting headteacher; from the outset the Associate Headteacher had to assume sole responsibility for three days a week. This also had to occur against a backdrop of special measures and the key objective to contribute to the removal of the school from the special measures category. The Associate Headteacher was once again an experienced deputy head from an adjoining borough seconded in a similar way, and for similar reasons to Case study A. His initial perceptions of the role were as follows: '*I believe that the most important factor in moving the school forward is creating the correct climate. Within this traditional setting the main task was to initiate a "can do" culture. The headteacher sets the tone for this.*'

As in Case study A, the relationship between the Associate and Executive Headteachers was paramount. This was mapped out at an early stage, based on the belief of both parties that there should be only one headteacher figure visible to the pupils, parents and staff. Therefore the Associate Headteacher took full responsibility for running the school, and in his own words 'all decisions and sometimes mistakes came from one person'.

This structure created:

- a clear leader;
- an experienced mentor with clear knowledge of both local education authority and headship matters;
- regular mentoring opportunities;
- coaching in specific developmental areas;
- a referral service for regular advice.

Given the context of special measures and the level of expectation in the school, while both the LEA and the MLC were content with the way the structures had been set up, further coaching support was identified through the inspectorate, and a member of the MLC team was appointed as a school governor. In-service training and professional development for senior and middle managers from the school was also provided by the MLC. Reflecting upon his experience, the Associate Headteacher feels that as well as the inputs from the local education authority and the MLC there could be a third element to this coaching and support.

> 'I believe that there should be a third part to this aspect whereby NCSL, HMI, and other local education authorities could offer without cost coaching on the effects of special measures and clear guidance on the management of change required. Contact with heads who had successfully managed this change and heads who were in similar circumstances would be extremely beneficial.'

There are some clear pointers within this statement for extending the principles of leadership coaching by collaboration. However, the extension to the collaborative networks suggested here would need further work to be done at both local and national level. The reference to the potential involvement of the NCSL is interesting, and perhaps as their regional centres develop (the MLC is a core partner in the West Midlands regional centre), this may be a role which they can fulfil.

As in Case study A, considerable forward momentum was generated within the school in a short period of time. Once again the governors and local education authority were keen to secure a substantive headteacher, who would be in post twelve months after the commencement of the secondment process. After the recruitment process the secondee was once again appointed as Headteacher of the school. He states that he would have been highly unlikely to have applied to this school in this local education authority, although at the time of his secondment he was actively seeking a headship. Being appointed on a permanent basis had an immediate impact upon perceptions within the school:

> 'I believe that from the outset I was perceived by both staff and governors as a new, young, inexperienced headteacher who had been placed in "their" school. . . . I applied for and obtained the substantive headship. This immediately removed much of the uncertainty and gave me a firmer standing on which to build future changes.'

The school continues to receive positive feedback from its HMI monitoring visits and will hopefully emerge from special measures during the prescribed two-year period. Several additional learning points have emerged from this case study. While the lack of an acting headteacher helped to avoid confusion from the outset, it does place considerable demands upon the secondee, which are similar to those faced by many newly appointed heads. The role of the executive headteacher differed in this case; they were far less 'hands on' and offered far more in the way of coaching and mentoring support. The placement of the school in special measures also meant that the decision to offer support via MLC input into the governors has also proved to be effective and useful. Governors have a key role to play in the recovery of the school, and it was crucial that they offered the secondee the maximum amount of support and encouragement. As in Case study A, in spite of the Acting Headteacher's exposure to, and participation in, leadership and management training there is no ultimate preparation for the rigours of headship. He offers the following thoughts based upon his experience:

> 'Practical hands-on experience is invaluable. More deputy heads should be given opportunities within their own school to take charge (for one or two terms). Heads could be seconded out to support intervention or school improvement strategies. This would be the most beneficial form of headship training – hands on. Total responsibility and a chance to make decisions that effect change.'

Conclusion

We are entering a new era within the leadership and management of schools and colleges. National professional development programmes coordinated by leadership colleges within each sector will continue to expose leading professionals to a wide range of in-service training. Furthermore, the pseudo-mandatory nature of some of these programmes will ensure that there is a consistent level of prescribed input into the training within the profession. Other training providers are refocusing their activities to enhance or embellish existing offerings, or are seeking gaps in the current market. The real growth appears to be within bespoke training for individuals, schools or groups of schools which are facing similar issues. The collaborations encouraged by the recent leadership incentive grants are encouraging groups of schools to work together to focus upon common development issues and activities. Similarly, the Specialist Schools Movement has recently introduced a programme of pairings which twin together high-achieving schools with others which are seeking improvement. While the research findings for this initiative are not yet available, some of these collaborations are dealing with discrete organisational issues, whereas others are clearly taking the form of a coaching model.

We are certainly moving beyond the position of headteachers and principals managing their schools and colleges in isolation, with what support that there was coming from local education authority inspectors or via professional organisations. The reduction in the scale and capacity of local education authorities and the autonomy granted to FE colleges left a vacuum which is now being filled by the introduction of the national leadership initiatives and which previously saw the growth of a large number of 'private training providers'. Coaching and mentoring are now part of the new collaborative and collegiate era in which we find ourselves, and as such are emerging as a crucial part of the support structures available to today's educationalists.

Extended activities

The remaining two 'extended' activities in this chapter are intended to further engage and challenge the reader with issues central to successful coaching, mentoring and peer-networking. Both of these activities draw upon case studies A and B shown earlier in this chapter. Although the case studies are drawn from the schools sector, the concepts of collaboration and executive coaching developed have clear resonance with leadership development within the further education sector. As such, the extended activities which follow are appropriate for readers from both schools and colleges. The first activity sets out to identify key features of leadership development emerging from Case study A. The second activity sets out to identify key features of leadership development emerging from Case study B.

Extended activity 6.7

An analysis of Case study A

Context

Reported in the case study. Please read Case study A.

Aims

- To identify key features of the development of leadership by collaboration within the case study.
- To identify key players within the collaboration.
- To consider the sustainability of the model and its possible transfer to your own professional context.
- To consider how the model might be improved.

---

continued

Steps

This activity consists of four steps. Steps may be undertaken by individuals working alone or in a group. Please read Case study A.

- *Step 1* involves identification of key features of the development of leadership by collaboration within the case study.
- *Step 2* involves identification of key players within the collaboration.
- *Step 3* involves consideration of the sustainability of the model and its possible transfer to your own professional context.
- *Step 4* involves consideration of how the model might be improved.

Step 1

List key features of the development of leadership by collaboration within the case study.

Step 2

Identify key players within the collaboration.

Step 3

Comment on the sustainability of the model and its possible transfer to your own professional context.

Step 4

How might the model be improved?

Extended activity 6.8

An analysis of Case study B

Context

Reported in the case study. Please read Case study B.

Aims

- To identify key features of the development of leadership by collaboration within the case study.
- To identify key players within the collaboration.
- To consider the sustainability of the model and its possible transfer to your own professional context.
- To consider how the model might be improved.

Steps

This activity consists of four steps. Steps may be undertaken by individuals working alone or in a group. Please read Case study B.

- *Step 1* involves identification of key features of the development of leadership by collaboration within the case study.
- *Step 2* involves identification of key players within the collaboration.
- *Step 3* involves consideration of the sustainability of the model and its possible transfer to your own professional context.
- *Step 4* involves consideration of how the model might be improved.

Step 1

List key features of the development of leadership by collaboration within the case study.

Step 2

Identify key players within the collaboration.

continued

Step 3

Comment on the sustainability of the model and its possible transfer to your own professional context.

Step 4

How might the model be improved?

Chapter 7

Raising performance and embedding change

Modelling the standards and assessing impact

Introduction

The national strategy for continuing professional development in the UK (see DfES, 2001a) strongly advocates the use of coaching, mentoring and peer-networking mechanisms to enhance teacher professional development and performance in schools. The same principles also apply within the college sector. It suggests that mutual support for learning, the dissemination of good practices, the translation of teacher learning to pupil learning and the embedding of desirable change are among the potential benefits to be realised from the adoption of such mechanisms (see DfES, 2001a, b, d; Harrison, 2001).

This chapter is concerned, therefore, with a consideration of mechanisms to embed changes in practice and the potential impact of such changes following teacher professional development. In particular, the chapter seeks to review how coaching and mentoring might assist in embedding change and effecting impact. Given that teachers are fully engaged by their professional development and professional learning occurs, will they encounter any difficulties in expressing their learning within their organisational context so as to effect improvement? Will professional learning have benefits for teachers at a personal and a professional level? Will they be able to express their learning so that it leads to positive impact on learners? Given that coaching and mentoring can assist in embedding change and enhancing the impact of professional learning, the need to define good standards of practice with respect to coaching and mentoring emerges. Formulating good standards has a direct bearing on the training of coaches and mentors, and offers a benchmark against which both teachers and organisational leaders can assess their practice so as to maximise potential advantages in deploying coaches and mentors within their organisations.

The role of coaching and mentoring in the induction of staff

The professional learning needs of experienced staff are different from those of newly qualified teachers. The effective induction of new staff is an important first step in ensuring that new colleagues are able to develop professionally and make an impact upon change and learning within classrooms at the earliest possible opportunity. In considering the mentoring of an experienced member of staff who is entering a new post, Fabian and Simpson (2002) point out that such teachers often have a wide range of knowledge about learning, and mentors need to acknowledge this and help to enable the expression of this expertise in a new role while developing the member of staff in new areas. Bleach (1999) suggests a continuum of help from enabling the new employee to become a member of the organisation to enabling the individual to develop according to his or her own strengths.

Earley and Kinder (1994) suggest four possible mentoring models:

1   The mono-support model identifies a single member of staff, usually a member of the senior management team, as being responsible for the central induction programme.
2   The bi-support model adds a mentor to the mono-support model for more direct day-to-day support of the inductee.

3   The tri-support model involves regular meetings with middle or senior managers as well as a mentor of a similar status as the inductee in the role of 'critical friend'.

4   The multi-support system whereby support is offered on a number of levels, from senior managers, middle managers, colleagues from the same year group or department as well as a mentor in the role of 'critical friend'.

Activity 7.1

Critically reflect on four mentoring models

Critically reflect on the four mentoring models provided.

• Does your organisation provide induction for new members of staff?
• Which of the four models is closest to that used in your own organisation?
• Which would potentially be the most effective to use within your own organisation?
• Who is responsible within your organisation for the induction of new staff?
• Is there a policy for induction within your organisation?
• How might that policy be improved?

Peer-coaching

In the United States of America, the term 'peer-coaching' is used to describe the relationship between teachers supporting teachers as they apply and reflect on new ways of teaching to better meet the needs of students. Peer-coaching may include out-of-class activities such as study groups and collaborative planning, and in-class coaching activities such as peer-observation.

Activity 7.2

Peer-observation

Peer-observation involves one teacher observing another colleague's practice and feeding back. As mutual trust underpins this kind of relationship, it works best when teachers choose to work together. Engage in a peer-observation relationship with a colleague. Decide together:

• What will be the focus of the observation (e.g. 'ending a lesson')?
• How will the observer behave (e.g. silent or participative)?
• How will the observer collect information to feed back?
• When and where will the feedback be given?
• How will reflection on practice be encouraged?
• What actions will follow to help improve practice?
• What observations are planned to give feedback on changing practice?

In-class coaching may take different forms depending on the purposes and goals of the coaching (see Swafford, 1998):

• *Technical coaching*: Involves the transfer of teaching methods introduced in workshops to the classroom.

- *Expert coaching*: Involves the use of teachers with expertise in particular methods who observe, support and provide feedback to other teachers.
- *Reciprocal coaching*: Involves teachers who observe and coach each other so that their practice may be improved.
- *Cognitive coaching*: Involves engaging teachers in ongoing dialogue about their classroom practices and exploring their meanings.

The form of coaching that will be most beneficial depends on the needs of particular teachers.

Activity 7.3

Different forms of peer-coaching

As part of professional development activities within the organisation, try and organise at least two of the above forms of coaching to take place with pairs of teachers who agree to take part.

- What feedback did you receive from the pairs?
- What were the benefits?
- What were the barriers?
- What is the potential for different forms of peer-coaching within your organisation?

In the United Kingdom, the DfES (2001a) suggests that:

> coaching and feedback on their [teachers'] professional practice over a period of weeks and months is a particularly important element, and can be decisive in determining whether changes in practice survive.

A helpful summary (see Table 7.1) of the relationship between the components of professional training and their impact on job performance based on the work of Joyce and Showers (1988) and Wallace (1996) is presented by West-Burnham and O'Sullivan (1998).

This emphasises the importance of coaching with respect to the transfer of skills and strategies to the classroom. Most performing occupations offer opportunities to observe skilled performers at work both before and after initial training, and also to discuss and share thoughts with such skilled mentors (see Eraut, 1994). Why then should teachers be denied such opportunities?

Table 7.1 The impact of coaching on the transfer of training to enhanced job performance

Training components and combinations	Impact on job performance
	Transfer
Theory	Nil
Theory and demonstration	Nil
Theory, demonstration and practice	Nil
Theory, demonstration, practice and feedback	Low
Theory, demonstration, practice, feedback and coaching	High

Source: Adapted from West-Burnham and O'Sullivan (1998)

Embedding change and the impact of professional learning on teachers

Teacher professional learning may result in a number of different outcomes which may have an impact on teachers at an individual level, at a classroom level or at an institutional level.

Kinder *et al.* (1991) have created a typology of In-Service Education and Training (INSET) outcomes:

- material and provisionary outcomes;
- information outcomes;
- new awareness;
- value congruence outcomes;
- affective outcomes;
- motivational and attitudinal outcomes;
- knowledge and skills;
- institutional outcomes;
- impact on practice.

Impact on teachers' practice may be influenced by any or all of these outcomes and impact should not be expressed exclusively in terms of quantifiable learning gains for pupils or students. Many authors suggest that teachers' insights and reflections on what constitutes significance and value in relation to their own personal, academic and professional needs and development are equally important outcomes. Given that teachers will have unique patterns of individual professional learning, Burchell *et al.* (2002) argue that there are different ways to demonstrate impact, and the articulation by teachers of the interplay between the hard, tangible outcomes of development and the affective, motivational outcomes rooted in personal and professional values is suggestive of professional development having taken place. Davies and Preston (2002) also emphasise the personal as well as the professional impact of professional development. The measurement of such impact is problematical.

Activity 7.4

Reflection on a professional development activity

Reflect critically on a professional development activity which has been influential to either or both your professional and personal development.

- What was the activity?
- What particular aspects of the activity were most influential to you?
- Was coaching, mentoring or peer-networking involved in effecting impact?
- How could you measure the extent of the impact upon yourself?
- Did the activity impact upon professional or personal development or both?
- What aspects would you suggest might be included in other professional development activities trying to achieve professional and/or personal impact with other colleagues?
- How might you act as a leader of learning for others?

Embedding change and the impact of professional learning on pupils and students

The ultimate aim of teacher professional learning is to impact positively on pupil or student learning (see Day, 1999; Bolam, 2000; Rhodes and Houghton-Hill, 2000), and it is to this aspect that the impact of professional learning is increasingly being linked. A code of practice for providers of professional development (DfES, 2001b) emphasises the need to maximise the impact of professional development by closely identifying development needs, meeting the needs of individual teachers and also linking the benefits of training to improvements to be experienced by pupils and students in the classroom.

However, impact in classrooms will not be attained unless sufficient support in the translation of teacher learning to pupil and student learning is effected. Barriers to the transfer of teacher learning to pupil learning have been shown to exist in some schools, and school managers themselves are implicated in the creation of such barriers (Rhodes and Houghton-Hill, 2000). School managers need to examine systems they themselves have created, which may impede the expression of teacher learning in classrooms.

This is born out by a recent Australian study (Peters, 2002) which suggested that participants' ability to translate their professional learning into educational improvement was related to the extent to which they individually and collectively felt empowered to address dilemmas and contextual constraints within their own organisations. The research indicated that many participants became aware of the dilemmas and constraints that existed in individual classroom contexts, and at the organisation and system level, which prevented them from achieving the goal of improvement in practices and contexts. Typical constraints were the syllabus, assessment and reporting demands, the negative attitudes of some staff and the ways schools structured time, roles, communication, decision-making and the allocation of resources. Dilemmas experienced by participants included knowledge as content versus knowledge as process, intrinsic versus extrinsic motivation, and learning is individual versus learning is social. Some felt obstacles to be insurmountable, at least in the short term, and their reform efforts foundered, while others became more determined to achieve reform and lobby for change. It seems that those in the latter group were supported by cultural factors such as working collaboratively on a common focus for reform and organisational leadership that was open to the need for contextual change to support reform.

Activity 7.5

Translating professional learning into educational improvement

Drawing on the above text, make a list of constraints and dilemmas impeding the translation of professional learning into educational improvement within your own organisation. What possible solutions may there be?

Guskey (1995) was critical of the measures used to judge the effectiveness of professional development and suggested that many evaluations measure participant satisfaction with professional development rather than changes in practice or impact on student learning. Peters (2002) suggested that the extent to which participants in professional development were able to determine whether educational improvement had occurred as a result of this development was related to agreement on what counts as improvement, strategies for assessment, feedback and review and time for reviewing outcomes. In an American study, Adelman and Panton Walking-Eagle (1997) found that reform initiatives often foundered once they had moved beyond the planning and initial stages of implementation. They attributed this failure to the fact that while additional time was usually made available for teachers to plan and begin to implement a reform initiative, this did not occur once the reform was seen to be underway. This meant that teachers who had trialed reforms did not have time to review outcomes, share successful practices and 'sell' the innovation.

Activity 7.6

Creating time for impact

Create the time to further develop, embed and evaluate changes in practice in terms of impact. Here are some suggestions to create time:

- timetable opportunities to collaborate with other colleagues;
- deploy cover staff;
- use professional development time for this purpose;
- establish coaching and mentoring time within the organisation;
- use some meeting time for this purpose.

Reflect critically the use of time within your own organisation. How can time savings be made? How can time savings be successfully used to support the embedding and impact of professional development? Analyse your suggestions in terms of the:

Suitability:	What suggestion is best in terms of grasping opportunities and exploiting strengths?
Feasibility:	Can the suggestion be implemented successfully?
Acceptability:	Is the suggestion acceptable to all of the stakeholders involved?

Training coaches and mentors – what are the standards?

It is suggested that the engagement of support using coaching, mentoring and networking activities may assist in the transfer of teacher learning to pupil and student learning, resulting in a greater impact within the classroom experience of learners and the increased potential to raise standards and attainment (see Joyce and Showers, 1988; Oldroyd and Hall, 1988; Wallace, 1996; Swafford, 1998; Rhodes and Houghton-Hill, 2000). Given that organisations spend significant sums of money on professional development with the intention of raising teacher performance (see Rhodes and Houghton-Hill, 2000; Rhodes, 2001), organisation leaders who are actively seeking the potential benefits of coaching, mentoring and peer-networking relationships will need to consider the placement of these mechanisms as part of normal working patterns in order to engender a climate of safety and trust.

Organisation leaders will also need to monitor and evaluate closely to assess the extent of any gains. Although not all staff are likely to be equally receptive as professional learners or suitable as coaches, mentors or peer-networkers, present lack of information and training in the UK (Harrison, 2001) is unhelpful in assisting organisations to take these mechanisms forward. Mentor training is available within some higher education institutions, and Garvey and Alred (2000) have made a survey of higher education attempts to address mentor education, concluding that the issue of mentor education is one which needs attention. It is strongly suggested that nationally or internationally agreed guidance concerning good practices in coaching, mentoring and peer-networking in education would be of use to teachers, organisation leaders, trainers and others concerned with the raising of standards and attainment in education. At least national standards are needed to make this a real and recognised and rewarding job.

Coaching and mentoring involve complex relationships demanding the highest levels of personal and professional competence. The following represents an attempt to specify standards appropriate to the work of both coaches and mentors. Suggesting standards in this way begs a number of assumptions. For example:

- standards are well conceived;
- individuals can attain the standards;
- individuals can be measured against the standards by someone competent to do so;
- that there is support to work towards the standards;
- that assessment can lead to failure as well as success in meeting the standards;
- while standards should not be compromised, they should allow for flexibility in how they are met given the differing work environments within teaching;
- that standards engender good practices which are transferable across the various sectors in education.

Standards are useful in defining what is expected of a coach or mentor, and ideally would be preceded by a needs analysis and objective setting prior to any training. In coaching and mentoring relationships there are clear knowledge, skill and human relations elements which must be taken into account, and training will inevitably require hands-on experience of coaching and/or mentoring. One way to develop standards is to relate them to 'responsibilities' associated with the tasks involved. Progress towards the standards would provide an important focus for professional development for the would-be coach or mentor. The role is wide-ranging, and at one extreme would require skills in inducting new staff and at the other entry into a long-term professional learning relationship with other colleagues.

Suggested standards appropriate to both coaches and mentors

Suggested standards fall under three broad headings. The order of standards shown under each heading does not imply an inherent hierarchy:

1 Develop and maintain effective and supportive relationships with adults

- They are able to show appropriate respect for adult learners.
- They are able to effect sensitive and non-judgemental communication and feedback.
- They are able to identify and understand the learning needs of others.
- They are able to engender trusting learning relationships which do not abuse power or indulge in excessive control.
- They are able to maintain learning relationships which do not allow excessive emotional dependence on either side.
- They are able to exhibit caring relationships which enable the learner to develop a feeling of professional self-worth.
- They are able to gain the respect for other staff through their effective practitionership.
- They are able to convey enthusiasm for learning and to motivate other adults to learn.
- They are able to serve as a role model but allow flexibility for learners to do things in other ways to which the mentor or coach may have 'always' done them.
- They are able to empower learners and provide continuing support for learners even if learners end up doing things better than the coach or mentor.
- They are self-confidently able to communicate clear personal attitudes and values.
- They are able to listen carefully to learners' concerns.
- They are able to be energetic, have a sense of humour and to avoid sarcasm or cynicism.
- They are able to be open to receive feedback themselves.
- They are able to ensure that learning experiences are not conceived of as an attack on learners' personal and/or professional competence.
- They are able to avoid oversimplification of complex issues so that the adult learners will not resist learning.

- They are able to apply techniques appropriate to adult learners who may be immediate colleagues.
- They are able to give credit to others for their ideas.

2 Manage and promote professional learning so as to enhance professional development provision

- They are able to promote collaborative and independent professional learning.
- They are able to promote positive values, attitudes and behaviour.
- They are able to work collaboratively and share good practices.
- They are able to develop learners as reflective practitioners.
- They are able to help others set targets for CPD.
- They are able to access appropriate resources.
- They are able to promote an open climate for exchange of ideas.
- They are able to contribute to the development of a collaborative CPD culture in the whole organisation.
- They are able to set challenging but achievable and realistic goals and targets which are measurable.
- They are able to enable others to improve their own performance.
- They are able to facilitate and embed changes in practice.
- They are able to express high expectations for themselves and for learners.
- They are able to make and implement professional learning plans.
- They are able to model continuous learning and reflection.
- They are able to balance support and enthusiasm with candour about current learner limitations.

3 Assimilate and apply knowledge and understanding appropriate to the role

- They are able to recognise their own role and place it in context within the organisation.
- They are able to deploy appropriate observational, listening, problem-solving and peer review skills.
- They are able to help others develop individual learning plans.
- They are able to give effective, constructive and non-judgemental feedback.
- They are able to apply techniques appropriate to adult learning and learning styles, and the motivation of adults to learn.
- They are able to sustain an appropriate locus of learning control within the organisation.
- They are able to undertake learning needs analysis.
- They are able in conjunction with organisation leaders to create learning time.
- They are able to express appropriate subject knowledge where this is important.
- They are aware of learning and career progression pathways for colleagues.
- They are able to handle data/evidence where this is necessary.
- They are aware of helpful external agencies.
- They are able to deploy appropriate monitoring and assessment of learners.
- They are able to report verbally and in writing to others with due regard for confidentiality.
- They are able to manage their own and others' time well.
- They are able to suggest out-of-work activities to consolidate and extend professional learning.
- They are able to support the principle of equality of opportunity.
- They are able to devise and apply the right questions to support learners' development.
- They are able to be aware politically within organisations and to know how things work and how things get done.

Extended activities

The remaining two 'extended' activities in this chapter are intended to further engage and challenge the reader with issues central to successful coaching, mentoring and peer-networking. The first activity sets out to explore criteria pertinent to the selection of coaches or mentors, and considers the pros and cons of engaging internal or external staff. The second activity enables the reader to explore possibilities and difficulties in the measurement of impact upon pupil or student learning resulting from teacher professional learning.

Extended activity 7.7

The appointment of a coach or mentor

Context

In seeking to train or appoint coaches or mentors, organisational leaders need to be clear about the purpose of the coaching or mentoring sought. What are eligibility requirements? What are criteria for nominating and selecting? Are there rewards for coaches and mentors? What are role boundaries? What is the professional identity of a coach or mentor? Are role and responsibilities clearly defined? Who are target individual(s) or group(s) to be coached or mentored? Is a suitable needs assessment of coaches and mentors in place? How will evaluation of the success of coaching and mentoring be undertaken? What happens after coaching and mentoring? How will the coach and mentor role be institutionalised? Is a policy in place? How will the budget be handled? How will the mentor/coach and their learners be matched? How will potential effectiveness of the programme be communicated? What are plans for short-term and long-term coach and mentor training? In short, how committed is the organisation?

Assuming commitment, appointment can then follow.

Aims

- To create a person specification prior to the appointment of a coach or mentor.
- To create interview questions to probe the suitability of potential candidates.
- To consider the benefits and disadvantages of internal or external appointments.

Steps

This activity consists of three steps. Steps may be undertaken by individuals alone or in a group.

- *Step 1* involves the creation of a person specification by drawing on information provided within the suggested standards with respect to coaches and mentors.
- *Step 2* involves the creation of interview questions, based on the suggested standards and person specification, in order to probe the likely suitability and effectiveness of would-be coaches and mentors.
- *Step 3* involves reflection on the pros and cons of selecting coaches and mentors from within the organisation as opposed to selection from outside the organisation.

continued

Step 1

Drawing on the suggested standards for coaches and mentors (above), devise a person specification for either a coach or a mentor. Try and express this in terms of 'essential' knowledge/skills/attributes and 'desirable' knowledge/skills/attributes.

Essential	Desirable

Step 2

Using the suggested standards and the person specification created in Step 1, devise a series of interview questions to probe the likely suitability and effectiveness of would-be coaches and mentors.

Step 3

Assess the pros and cons of seeking to appoint coaches and mentors from within the organisation rather than from outside the organisation (e.g. an LEA adviser or an independent consultant). You could use a table like this one.

Pros	Cons

Conclusion:

Extended activity 7.8

Measuring the impact on pupils/students following teacher professional development

Context

Can teacher learning be translated into the classroom experience of pupils and students? How does one measure this? Flecknoe (2000) has suggested that it was possible to show that some teachers who had attended a professional development programme to learn about school improvement, school effectiveness and action research did enhance pupil achievement following a specific intervention within their own schools designed specifically for this purpose. Although this result was partially confounded by the fact that the teachers engaged with the professional development may have been sufficiently interested in school improvement that they would have raised attainment anyway. Nevertheless, many of the teachers were convinced that positive gains in pupil attitude or achievement had been made as a result of the professional development they had received.

It is widely recognised in the literature that one of the greatest challenges for those working to reform educational practice is trying to determine whether improvement has occurred. While at government level CPD has become a major part of the education improvement agenda, it has brought with it government concern that there should be value for money and some signs of 'impact'. Measuring impact in terms of a clear linkage between CPD and raised attainment in classrooms, given the multitude of other possible intervening variables, makes such a measurement particularly problematic. Although not all professional development will lend itself to direct classroom intervention, the requirement for linkage between professional development and demonstrable classroom improvement is firmly established. This establishment is strengthened by research literature which places a firm focus on teacher and pupil/student learning within classrooms in the drive to attain maximum improvement benefits resulting in raised achievement for all (see Harris and Hopkins, 1999; Rhodes and Houghton-Hill, 2000).

Aims

- To seek direct gains in pupil/student achievement linked to CPD activity.
- To reflect critically on the difficulties and possible solutions to linking CPD and gains in pupil/student achievement.
- To establish protocols for identifying and measuring such linkage which may be of use to others within the organisation.

Steps

This activity may be undertaken individually or as part of a group. It assumes that recent professional development activity has taken place and that this professional development is such that it has the potential to impact positively on the achievement of pupils or students in the classroom.

- *Step 1* involves identifying a recent professional development activity so that it may form the focus of efforts to link this experience to the enhanced classroom achievement of individual pupils/students or groups of pupils/students. Try to create a list to show potential facilitators or potential barriers to the translation of your professional development to impact within the classroom experience of pupils/students.
- *Step 2* involves establishing how you will assess pupils/students to measure any gains in achievement. It also involves making a plan to create the time to undertake the

continued

measurement, collect evidence and reflect upon it so as to judge whether any positive changes have occurred.

- *Step 3* involves creation of a summary of your experiences so that any demonstration of impact within the classroom may be made available to others. This availability may enable them to effect improvement themselves by implementing your own changes, or by encouraging them to undertake measurements of their own with respect to their own professional development experiences.

Step 1

Choose a recent professional development experience which offers you the opportunity to link your professional learning to the classroom experience of pupils or students. Undertake an intervention based on this learning intended to raise achievement for individual pupils/ students or groups of pupils/students. Complete a list to examine facilitators and barriers to linkage of your learning to the classroom experience of your chosen pupil(s) or student(s).

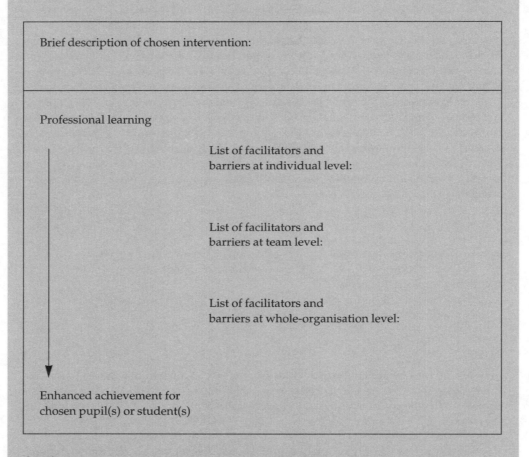

Brief description of chosen intervention:

Professional learning

List of facilitators and
barriers at individual level:

List of facilitators and
barriers at team level:

List of facilitators and
barriers at whole-organisation level:

Enhanced achievement for
chosen pupil(s) or student(s)

Step 2

Use the following pro forma, which may be modified should you wish, to focus on your intervention. Establish the method(s) of assessment you will use in order to collect evidence about possible gains in specified pupil(s) or student(s) achievement. Consider time implications of the proposed measurement and evidence collection. Reflect upon what you have found with respect to any positive change.

Pro forma

Cognitive gains (measurable academic learning)
Have the specified pupils/students experiencing the intervention made more progress than another group with no intervention? Than the equivalent group last year? Than would have been expected from targets set? From previous rates of progress?

Evidence:

Affective gains (measurable behaviour, relationships, atmosphere)
Have specified pupils/students experiencing the intervention demonstrated more positive attitude and behaviours?

Evidence:

No gains recorded

Has the intervention yielded no evidence concerning positive changes? Has the intervention resulted in a worsening of attainment and/or behaviour?

Evidence:

Step 3

Summarise your findings for others, using the following headings:

Professional development accessed:

Brief description of intervention:

Specified pupil(s)/student(s):

Improvement sought:

Assessment/measurement used:

continued

Time implications:

Facilitators:

Barriers:

Findings:

Recommendations for the future:

Additional notes:

Chapter 8

Overcoming barriers

Leadership and management issues in coaching, mentoring and peer-networking

Introduction

Coaching and mentoring activities required close partnership between colleagues within an environment of trust, safety, support and mutual respect (see Ponzio, 1987; Tharp and Gallimore, 1988; West-Burnham and O'Sullivan, 1998; Harris, 2000, 2001; Thompson, 2001). Importantly, it has been established that teacher collaboration is necessary for professional learning to occur (Harris, 2000). Implementation of coaching, mentoring and networking, and the creation of an environment in which mutual support can flourish may present challenges within some schools and colleges. For example, West-Burnham and O'Sullivan (1998) highlight the need for high-quality personal and interpersonal skills, mutual trust, confidence and respect within successful coaching relationships. However, it is known that collaboration between individuals so that they can work and learn together is not prevalent in many schools (see Harris, 2001). In some schools, where collaboration is established, benefits in terms of enhanced professional development have been recorded. For example, Beatty (2000) has shown that self-directed professional learning, personal and shared reflection, and authentic collaboration in a supportive study group environment can create changes in teachers' perceptions of themselves and their work and catalyse professional growth. A report by Day *et al.* (2002) has suggested that provision of opportunities to teachers to reflect on their teaching and engage in dialogue with other teachers about it can help to build motivation and commitment. Given that teacher collaboration and mutual support offer the potential to raise teacher confidence and facilitate professional learning (see Rhodes and Beneicke, 2002), leadership teams need to consider how productive collaboration can be engendered within the context of their own organisations, how they might remove obstacles to sharing and how they may offer support as well as challenge. Emphasising the importance of leadership with respect to the outcomes experienced by teachers engaging in professional development, Earley *et al.* (2002) have recommended that a key component of leadership training programmes should include managing professional development for others as well as inclusion of theoretical frameworks which underpin professional learning. Leaders can influence the culture and purpose of their organisations and, as such, they are able to create an environment which can influence job-related attitudes.

Activity 8.1

Leadership for professional learning

Make a list of as many statements as you can to illustrate how leadership impacts upon your own professional learning (e.g. involvement in decision-making).
    Reflect on these statements.

* Which do you consider to be positive impacts?
* Which do you consider to be negative impacts?

Leaders can influence the emotional climate of their organisations and, in so doing, motivate staff and impact positively upon teachers' working lives. Evans (2001) suggests that leadership can shape work contexts that either match or are at odds with what individuals want in relation to equity and justice, pedagogy or androgogy, organisational efficiency, interpersonal relations, collegiality and self-conception and self-image. In summary, leaders can make significant interventions to enhance the working lives of teachers within schools and colleges.

Activity 8.2

Emotional climate and performance

Emotional climate within the organisation (how individuals feel) can influence their performance for good or for ill. For example, emotions such as fear and anxiety can act to limit performance, whereas emotions such as optimism and self-esteem can serve to drive performance.

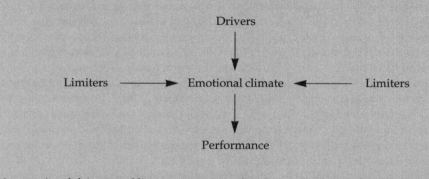

List emotional drivers and limiters experienced within your own professional context.

- How can leadership act to increase drivers?
- How can leadership act to decrease limiters?

Barriers to the impact of professional development in the classroom

In a study undertaken in the UK, Rhodes and Houghton-Hill (2000) found that although mechanisms for dissemination or cascading of the outcomes of CPD were reported in the overwhelming majority of schools included in the study, confidence in these mechanisms varied considerably. It was found that the outcomes of professional development were reported most frequently through departmental meetings. Similarly, departmental and faculty reviews were heavily relied upon to evaluate the impact of CPD within classrooms. It is likely that CPD dissemination mechanisms in some colleges are also similarly flawed. The supportive role of departmental heads is likely to be essential if transmission of change to the classroom experience of pupils and students is to be effected and ensured. Given the reliance placed on middle managers for the facilitation of transfer of teacher learning to the classroom and the evaluation of its success in terms of enhanced learning, senior managers need to be additionally vigilant that good intentions are not lost at this stage of transfer. An investigation by Wikeley (1998) offered the suggestion that senior managers should consider becoming more involved at departmental-level meetings, thereby facilitating the transfer of learning to classrooms through enhanced collaboration, monitoring and discussion. In organisations where the transmission of teacher learning to the classroom experience of learners is not assured, senior managers themselves may therefore represent a barrier to impact and need to review their practices. Over half the senior managers interviewed in the study undertaken by Rhodes and Houghton-Hill (2000) espoused the importance of extending in-house development of new ideas so as to increase the likelihood of lasting change. A barrier here is the lack of teacher collaboration and support from a coach, mentor or peer group in realising impact in the classroom.

The encouragement of additional in-house collaboration, discussion, mentoring, coaching and peer support through a culture of collegiality may yield significant benefits in some schools and colleges. Action to identify and break barriers to the impact of professional development on the classroom experience of pupils and students in individual schools and colleges is essential.

With respect to the impact of CPD within the classroom experience of pupils and students, teacher learners need to make appropriate and relevant connections between their learning and its application. It is likely that experienced teachers can do this more quickly than less experienced teachers. Well-organised prior knowledge gained through experience which is readily related to a particular professional context should enable transfer to occur more easily. For this reason, experienced teachers working out of their sphere of prior experience and familiar context as well as less experienced teachers will need access to coaching, mentoring and networking.

Activity 8.3

Reflexivity

The role of experience as a source of practitioners' learning is well established. As learning occurs, practitioners' horizons will shift, and as they look back they can view their learning journey. They can see how they have come to talk differently, how they have come to act differently. This looking back can be called reflexivity. It is a gateway to new learning and future changes in practice.

Look back over the past year of your professional practice. What learning have you assimilated which has now become part of your professional practice? What are the new contexts in which you are now applying this learning?

Are you able to draw a time line to show new learning and its application?

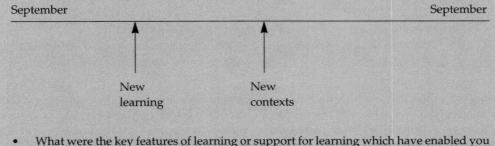

| September | September |

- What were the key features of learning or support for learning which have enabled you to embed this learning in your practice?
- How can facilitation of this transfer from learning to practice be recreated for you again?

The changing nature of leadership?

There is a growing realisation that 'distributed leadership' is crucial to institutional success. In some organisations, leadership is now indeed moving towards a broader concept that suggests responsibility for a shared purpose of community. However, distribution of leadership in some organisations may prove challenging. For example, the hierarchical nature of many schools and colleges is well established, and although there is variation, leadership tends to reside with the headteacher or principal and other members of the senior management team. In a leadership survey by Hay McBer (2000), headteachers were characterised as follows:

> Headteachers fall into the 85th percentile of the population for use of a coercive style. They are prone, as a group, to issuing orders and expecting obedience. While this can help create clarity and raise standards in the short term, over the long term it diminishes responsibility and team commitment.

Law (1999) has pointed to the need for approachable operational leaders within organisations who have qualities which define them as 'someone who understands the problems we are facing' rather than acting as leadership agents within an instrumentalist and managerialist educational environment. In any organisation, leadership may draw upon 'managerialist' (broadly speaking, directive and top-down leadership) or 'democratic' (broadly speaking, collegiate and consultative leadership) perspectives.

The work of Sachs (2001) which discusses teacher professional identities highlights the nature of these perspectives:

1   The managerialist discourse gives rise to an 'entrepreneurial' identity in which the market and issues of accountability, economy, efficiency and effectiveness shape how teachers individually and collectively construct their professional identities.
2   The democratic discourse gives rise to an 'activist' professional identity in which collaborative cultures are an integral part of teachers' work practices. Democratic discourses provide the conditions for the development of communities of practice.

Activity 8.4

Teacher identities

Does leadership within your own professional context lead to teacher self-perception in terms of accountability, economy, efficiency and effectiveness or self-perception in terms of collaboration and membership of a community of practice, or both?

- How does this impact upon the embedding of changes in practice?
- How does this impact upon the emergence of coaching, mentoring and peer-networking?

An important role of leadership in school or college improvement is to act as a catalyst in creating a learning environment for both teachers and learners (see Harris and Lambert, 2003a). Schools and colleges aspiring to be learning organisations need to take seriously the creation of healthy and successful learning environments for everyone within the organisation (see Bredeson, 2000).

Activity 8.5

Learning environments

- How might the creation of successful learning environments for adults in the school or college result in successful learning for pupils and students?
- What strategies are available to support staff in addressing problems they encounter in their teaching?

- What activities are available to foster teachers' thinking and practice?
- Are all staff involved in such activities?
- How well are teachers' learning activities linked to organisational development practices?

What can leaders do to improve professional development and its impact?

Clement and Vandenberghe (2001) pose a number of direct questions:

1   How do teachers assess the school leader's influence on their professional development and what meaning do they attach to their school leader's influence on their professional development?
2   How can we understand the impact of the school leader on this process? Through which specific processes and mechanisms do the workplace conditions that school leaders create contribute to teachers' professional development?

They conclude that the workplace conditions which foster professional learning reflect the creation of learning opportunities and the learning space to work with these opportunities.

Dufour and Berkey (1995) suggest ten ways in which principals can promote organisational development by focusing on teacher professional development:

1   create consensus about the organisation and what it is trying to become;
2   identify, promote and protect shared values;
3   monitor the critical elements of the organisation improvement effort;
4   ensure systematic collaboration throughout the organisation;
5   encourage experimentation;
6   develop a commitment to professional growth;
7   provide one-to-one staff development;
8   provide staff development programmes that are purposeful and research-based;
9   promote individual and organisational self-efficacy;
10 stay committed to continuous improvement and the goal of becoming a learning organisation.

In summary, with respect to the translation of teacher learning into changes in classroom practices, leadership can provide advocacy, targeted funds and other resources, be a broker of targeted support, monitor progress and protect teachers from competing demands and premature expectations of success.

Bredeson and Johansson (2000) identify four areas where principals have the opportunity to make a substantial impact on teacher learning:

1   The principal as an instructional leader and learner (steward, model, expert, instructional leader).
2   The creation of a learning environment (communicate, support, manage).
3   Direct involvement in the design, delivery and content of professional development (aligning professional development with school goals and teacher needs, empowering teachers as decision-makers, identifying needs, developing ongoing planning processes, creating dialogues on teachers' professional development, supporting a variety of learning opportunities for teachers, keeping the focus on student learning).
4   The assessment of professional development outcomes (help set and obtain feedback on professional learning and improvement goals, identify teachers' needs and collaboratively plan with teachers to provide expertise and resources).

Although research to elucidate how schools and colleges become effective learning communities is still underway, it is clear that a major role for leaders in the area of teacher professional development is to build leadership capacity among staff within their organisations so as to create an authentic learning community.

Activity 8.6

A model for leadership

Write bullet points to illustrate your own ideal model for leadership support required to advance your own professional learning and career development. Include points on your relationship with your team leader or line manager and how this person may offer support appropriate to your needs.

Consider your empowerment as a professional learner and how this empowerment may lead to both personal and professional impact.

What are the similarities and differences between your ideal model and your current professional experiences?

Extended activities

The remaining two 'extended' activities in this chapter are intended to further engage and challenge the reader with issues central to successful coaching, mentoring and peer-networking. The first activity sets out to explore context, processes and systems within the organisation which may hinder or facilitate the transmission of teacher learning to pupil or student learning. In so doing, readers are invited to rank-order their findings using the criteria of economy, efficiency, effectiveness and mutability. Finally, recommendations are sought to inform leadership action concerning the better facilitation of the transfer of teacher learning to pupil or student learning. The second activity enables readers to explore an organisational and leadership vision for coaching, mentoring and peer-networking intended to involve other staff in these mechanisms.

Extended activity 8.7

Tackling barriers to the impact of CPD in the classroom

Context

The UK government has suggested that teaching needs to become a learning profession. A link has been forged between teachers professional learning and the desirability of expression of that learning within the classroom. The transmission of teacher learning to raise standards and attainment for pupils and students has been described as the prime purpose of teacher professional development. However, issues begin to emerge; for example, how do organisations ensure, monitor and evaluate such impact and what barriers to impact exist in individual organisations? Given that many organisations spend large sums of money on teacher professional development with the intention of raising teacher and learner performance, what value for money does this spend provide if there are significant barriers to impact within the classroom experience of learners? What barriers are caused by activities and systems pertaining to leadership and what actions can organisation leaders take to diminish or remove such barriers?

According to Power (1997), 'value for money' audit claims to evaluate performance according to different sorts of criteria:

- *Economy* – the acquisition of resources on the best possible terms;
- *Efficiency* – the use of resources to achieve a given level of output;
- *Effectiveness* – the match between intentions and outcomes;
- *Mutability* – used in this context as a measure of the embeddedness within the current culture and the difficulty perceived in changing this context, process or system. High mutability corresponds to ease of change.

Aims

- To consider context, processes and systems within the organisation which may hinder or facilitate the transmission of teacher learning to pupil or student learning.
- To rank order context, processes and systems according to their cause for concern within the organisation on the basis of economy, efficiency, effectiveness and mutability.
- To recommend leadership actions to improve context, processes and systems so that they may better facilitate the transmission of teacher learning to pupil or student learning.

Steps

This activity consists of three steps. Steps may be undertaken by individuals working alone or in a group.

- *Step 1* involves reflection on context, processes and systems within the organisation which may hinder or facilitate the transmission of teacher learning to pupil or student learning.
- *Step 2* involves rank ordering identified context, processes and systems according to their economy, efficiency, effectiveness and mutability.
- *Step 3* involves the formulation of recommendations for leadership action as a result of reflection and subsequent scoring.

Step 1

Use the following list of questions pertaining to possible context, processes and systems supplemented by others emerging from your own organisation and decide whether they mostly facilitate or hinder the transmission of teacher learning to pupil or student learning.

1 How is the overall effectiveness of professional development evaluated within your school or college?
   Does this mostly facilitate or hinder transmission?   Y/N

2 Is evaluation concerned with participant satisfaction or with changes in practice or impact on pupil/student learning?
   Does this mostly facilitate or hinder transmission?   Y/N

3 How are the outcomes of professional development disseminated within your school or college?
   Does this mostly facilitate or hinder transmission?   Y/N

4 Is networking of any kind available so that learning may be shared rather than just disseminated?
   Does this mostly facilitate or hinder transmission?   Y/N

continued

5   How does the organisation evaluate the effect of professional development in the classroom?
    Does this mostly facilitate or hinder transmission?   Y/N

6   Do you feel empowered individually to address dilemmas and constraints within the school or college so that professional development may be translated into classroom improvements?
    Does this mostly facilitate or hinder transmission?   Y/N

7   Do you feel empowered collectively to address dilemmas and constraints within the organisation so that professional development may be translated into classroom improvements?
    Does this mostly facilitate or hinder transmission?   Y/N

8   Are teachers sufficiently autonomous or too role constrained to take decisions and/or actions so that professional development may be translated into classroom improvements?
    Does this mostly facilitate or hinder transmission?   Y/N

9   Is there reliance on middle managers to take the lead so that professional development may be translated into classroom improvements?
    Does this mostly facilitate or hinder transmission?   Y/N

10 Does the leadership in your organisation welcome changes in context, processes and systems to support change resulting from professional development?
    Does this mostly facilitate or hinder transmission?   Y/N

11 How helpful is the prevailing climate of collaboration within the organisation?
    Does this mostly facilitate or hinder transmission?   Y/N

12 Do other colleagues take the role of supporting coach or mentor?
    Does this mostly facilitate or hinder transmission?   Y/N

13 How difficult is it to raise motivation among immediate colleagues?
    Does this mostly facilitate or hinder transmission?   Y/N

14 How difficult is it to raise motivation among leaders?
    Does this mostly facilitate or hinder transmission?   Y/N

15 What time is allowed to help implement, embed and evaluate changes in practice which may impact on pupil/student learning?
    Does this mostly facilitate or hinder transmission?   Y/N

16 How difficult is it to obtain the resources required to help embed changes in practice which may impact on pupil/student learning?
    Does this mostly facilitate or hinder transmission?   Y/N

17 Add other questions pertaining to processes and systems within your school or college.
    Do these mostly facilitate or hinder transmission?   Y/N

Step 2

Use the list of questions and your answers pertaining to possible context, processes and systems supplemented by any others emerging from your own organisation from Step 1 and rank-order them according to your perception of their economy, efficiency, effectiveness and mutability. The higher rankings show good economy, good efficiency, good effectiveness and good mutability.

Rank order (1–16+) for economy:

Rank order (1–16+) for efficiency:

Rank order (1–16+) for effectiveness:

Rank order (1–16+) for mutability:

Which particular contexts, processes or systems are showing low rankings for economy, efficiency and effectiveness? Which of these will be difficult to change according to their low mutability ranking?

Step 3

Use your high rankings from Step 2 to establish present good practices in the translation of teacher learning to pupil/student learning. Use your low rankings from Step 2 to formulate a short report for a chosen audience to illustrate barriers and difficulties to the impact of CPD in the classroom. Highlight where leadership action may be needed if particular items are showing themselves to be perceived as relatively immutable.

Extended activity 8.8

A vision for coaching, mentoring and peer-networking: involving staff in the process

Context

Coaching, mentoring and peer-networking to effect professional development and increase performance have been shown to have positive effects within the business community if appropriately led and managed. For example, in a review of 151 articles relating to business mentoring, Hansford *et al.* (2002) found a wide range of positive learner outcomes such as motivation, enhanced skills and improved performance. These researchers also found a wide range of positive organisational outcomes such as staff retention, increased productivity and promotion of team spirit.

The work of Gunter and Ribbins (2003) examines the idea of effective school leadership from conceptual, descriptive, humanistic, critical, evaluative and instrumental points of view. How might such an analysis point to effective leadership for the involvement of staff in coaching, mentoring and peer-networking? Can such an analysis help to inform a leadership vision for coaching, mentoring and peer-networking?

continued

Aims

- To analyse the idea of effective leadership for the involvement of staff in coaching, mentoring and peer-networking.
- To draw on this analysis in order to inform leadership vision and action with respect to coaching, mentoring and peer-networking.

Steps

This activity consists of two steps. Steps may be undertaken by individuals working alone or in a group.

- *Step 1* involves an analysis of effective leadership for the involvement of staff in coaching, mentoring and peer-networking by drawing on the knowledge provinces of educational leadership as defined in the work of Gunter and Ribbins (2003).
- *Step 2* involves the construction of a leadership vision/action plan with respect to the involvement of others in coaching, mentoring and peer-networking.

Step 1

Use the following analysis in order to formulate your own responses to the notion of effective leadership for the involvement of other staff in coaching, mentoring and peer-networking. The analysis uses a modification of the schema presented by Gunter and Ribbins (2003).

Conceptual:
- What does it mean to involve others?

Descriptive:
- What do those involved do?
- What do those who seek to involve others do?

Humanistic:
- What knowledge already exists of being involved in these mechanisms?
- What knowledge already exists of involving others in these mechanisms?

Critical:
- Who should be included?
- Who should be excluded?
- How does this impinge upon structures and relationships within the organisation?

Evaluative:
- What impact on individual outcomes might occur if these staff are involved?
- What impact on organisational outcomes might occur if these staff are involved?

Instrumental:
- What are the best strategies to use in order to involve others in these mechanisms?

Your own responses in answer to this analysis:

Conceptual:

Descriptive:

Humanistic:

Critical:

Evaluative:

Instrumental:

Step 2

Use your responses from Step 1 to construct a leadership vision/action plan with respect to the involvement of others in coaching, mentoring and peer-networking.

Can you reduce the information contained within your responses into a unifying, understandable and communicable vision statement which points the way forward to the achievement of the involvement of other staff in coaching, mentoring and peer-networking?

Vision statement

Can you use information contained within your responses to construct an action plan with respect to the involvement of others in coaching, mentoring and peer-networking?

Action plan

Objective:

continued

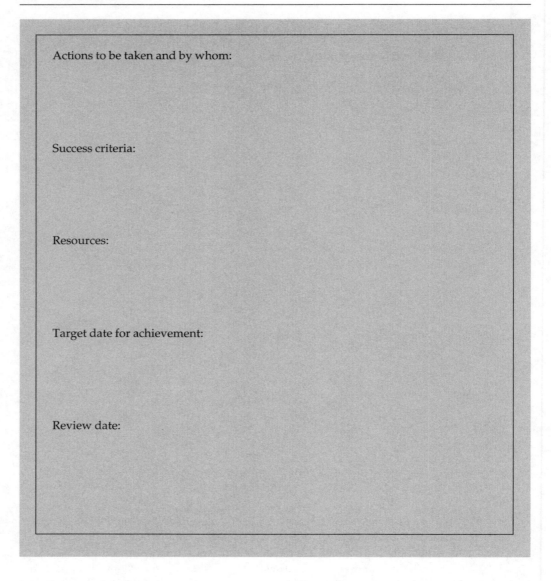

Chapter 9

Towards a professional learning community

A new strategy for professional development

Introduction

A relationship between the professional learning of employees and 'continuous' improvement has been established in commercial organisations for many years. Those organisations aspiring to use ongoing professional learning to deal with rapidly changing internal and external work environments have come to be known as 'learning organisations'. The use of professional learning to effect successful change has been frequently couched in terms such as 'organisational transformation', 'improved competitive advantage' and 'organisational survival'. For example:

> a learning organisation facilitates the learning of all of its members and continuously transforms itself.
>
> (Pedler *et al.*, 1988)

> learning has become the key developable and tradeable commodity of an organisation. Generating and selling the know-how and know-why, the learning of the organisation and its people, is becoming the core of any organisation which has a chance of surviving in the longer term.
>
> (Garratt, 1987)

> to respond to rapidly changing environments and markets, organisations need to learn at least as quickly as the prevailing rate of change, otherwise they are forever playing catch-up.
>
> (O'Sullivan, 1997)

To help understand how a learning organisation works in practice, Senge (1992) offers the following description aimed at team level:

> Most of us at one time or another, have been part of a great team, or group of people who functioned together in an extraordinary way – who trusted each other, who complemented each other's strengths and weaknesses and compensated for each other's limitations, who had common goals that were larger than individual goals and who produced extraordinary results. I have met many people who have experienced this sort of profound teamwork. What they experienced was a learning organisation.

In essence, an organisation concerned with supporting professional learning, engaging in critical self-reflection and sharing learning to bring about improvement, may be viewed as an aspiring learning organisation. The re-invention of schools as learning organisations has become part of the national school professional development agenda in the United Kingdom. The national strategy for continuing professional development for teachers (see DfES, 2001a) asks all headteachers and their leadership teams to think about how to make their school a real learning community. This has been reinforced recently in a consultation document emerging from the DfES (2003) which proposes a series of core principles for school improvement. Among these principles, schools are asked to give consideration to the creation of 'time for staff to learn together, to make performance more consistent and effective across the school'. The consultation document suggests:

There is much greater variation in performance on teaching and learning within schools than between them. Tackle this by creating a professional learning community, with time and opportunities for input on subject specialism and pedagogy, and for teachers and other staff in and beyond the school to work together across the curriculum to share good practice, hone their knowledge and skills, and develop their confidence in different ways of teaching. Link this to the performance management process, and use activities such as collective enquiry, peer observation and coaching, since these are likely to have the maximum impact on teachers' classroom practice.

A study of professional development in further education by the FEFC (1999) Inspectorate identified that: 'The best colleges have well-organised staff development systems managed by an individual with a dedicated role.'

This is not the image of a learning organisation, where at least team leaders see themselves as leaders of professional development in which every member of staff is empowered to engage in professional learning. Research by Peeke (2002) suggests that:

CPD in the college setting can be considered to include study for further qualifications, in-college development programmes of a formal or more informal nature such as mentoring, coaching and networking, and learning from experience.

Such CPD has now been given an official boost by being identified as an important part of college three-year development plans (see LSC, 2003). It was also noted in the LSC (2003) document that: 'As yet there is no nationally agreed definition of what constituted continuous professional development [CPD].' Perhaps colleges as well as schools should be encouraged to become learning organisations.

Given a national policy focus on teachers' learning and development, and given that access to professional learning depends upon the culture and circumstances of the particular organisation in which teachers happen to be working, what characteristics of a learning organisation does your own organisation display?

Activity 9.1

Characteristics of a learning organisation

MacBeath (2001) offers the following insight into the characteristics of a learning organisation. If Ofsted were to become a learning organisation it would:

- acknowledge the authority and wisdom of teachers;
- listen to the greater understanding of its critics;
- broaden the scope of its thinking;
- be self-evaluating – taking feedback on its own effectiveness from management, teachers and pupils;
- contextualise its findings;
- discuss its findings in a reflective, critical and evidence-based way so as to provide a learning experience for the school and for Ofsted;
- help lead to capacity-building;
- help in learning to know what we see rather than seeing what we already know.

Use this list to reflect upon the characteristics of a learning organisation which your own organisation already shows or needs to develop.

The DfES (2001a) reports that some school learning communities are already known to exist and seem to have a mix of some or all of the following four factors:

1   The vision and commitment of the headteacher, supported by the senior management team, placing professional development of their staff at the heart of school improvement.
2   The use of the Investors in People framework, or occasionally one of the other 'excellence' models, to underpin their approach to staff development.
3   Imaginative ways of organising the school, timetabling lessons and using resources to create time and opportunity for professional development, sometimes combined with access to, or the ability to generate, additional resources.
4   Participation in networks and partnerships which are a significant source of additional ideas and learning opportunities for their staff.

Such a model of a learning community is also applicable to colleges. Although not expressed in terms of 'learning communities' within the further education sector, a desire to 'embed a culture of continuous improvement and innovation in all providers, building on the strong commitment that already exists' (DfES, 2002) is recognised.

How well is organisational learning developed in your own school or college?

Activity 9.2

Organisational learning

Swieringa and Wierdsma (1992) have developed a model to understand organisational learning based on three levels:

1   single-loop learning – where the focus is on improving the rules, and solutions are within existing insights and principles;
2   double-loop learning – where there is a renewal of the insights within existing principles;
3   triple-loop learning – where there is the development of new principles which fundamentally question values and goals (need good communications which will enable perceptions and images of new organisational behaviour to be shared).

Within your professional experience in your own organisation can you identify any single-loop, double-loop or triple-loop learning? Which type of learning is the most prevalent? Where does the drive for learning come from? Do you share the outcomes of learning with others? What does this tell you about professional learning within your own organisation?

Capacity and performance

Professional learning communities are not born in their final state; they are nurtured and sustained by the value their members derive from them. The importance of leadership commitment to professional learning as a lever to organisational improvement is reviewed by Jackson and Payne (2002):

In the literature from the 'learning organisations field', it is viewed that leaders are stimulators (who get things started); they are story tellers (to encourage dialogue and aid understanding); they are networkers and problem solvers too. They tend to value a wider social repertoire than has been customary in hierarchical educational settings, in order to encourage openness and to foster and support relationships during times when members are wrestling with ambiguity.

They will build trust. They will model improvisation and be comfortable with risk-taking and spontaneity. They will also care, deeply, about teachers and about children and about education because that is the source of emotional energy for others. Intriguingly, they will be less personally ambitious, perhaps a long time in post, and will instead be remorseless about improvement. As leaders, they will place priority on the school as a context for adult learning. They will support staff at all levels to be able to make more sense of and interpret the emerging circumstances of school improvement.

Ensuring staff learning through knowledge-creating activities is an important means by which leaders can create the capacity for organisational improvement. Leaders can foster teachers' learning with and from other teachers in the interests of the pupils and students. Effective leaders are able, among other things, to empower staff by developing a climate of collaboration (see Day *et al.*, 2001). Harris and Lambert (2003b) also emphasise the role of leaders in capacity-building for improvement within their organisations and suggest the importance of the creation of learning environments in which all staff can share in distributed learning and improvement efforts:

> Effective school leaders build the capacity for improvement within their schools. They generate the conditions and create the climate for improvement to be initiated and sustained. Effective leaders orchestrate rather than dictate improvement and create learning communities within their schools. The role of leadership in school improvement is primarily to act as a catalyst in creating a learning environment for both teachers and pupils. This necessarily involves building the capacity within the school for learning and improvement to take place. Schools that 'build capacity' for implementing change are more likely to sustain improvement over time. In other words, they are able to generate both the readiness to change and the internal capacity to manage the change process.

Knowing how to establish a professional learning community within their organisation is an important attribute for all leaders, and the development of such knowledge should perhaps constitute part of leadership training.

Activity 9.3

Strategies to promote learning

What strategies and processes can you identify which would help school or college communities to work together to promote individual, collective and organisational learning?

According to Law and Glover (1996), those organisations which manage their professional development most effectively are those most frequently using five fundamental organisational elements in order to manage a secure and supportive professional development culture:

1   the effective management of information flows;
2   the development of shared and open planning processes;
3   the operation of clear resource allocation procedures with focused aims and targets;
4   the establishment of clear evaluation strategy used as a basis for ongoing review and development;
5   the development of open networking opportunities to facilitate mutual support and reflection.

Despite the important role of headteachers and college principals, the facilitation of professional learning is not the sole prerogative of leaders at this level. Other leaders, such as team leaders, and

Activity 9.4

Policies for a learning community

What policies exist in your organisation which encourage people involved in the life of the organisation to become part of the whole organisation learning community?

- Teachers?
- Other school or college staff?
- Pupils/students?
- Parents?
- Governors?
- LEA?
- Business?
- Wider community?

Where are the strengths? Where are the weaknesses?

teachers as adult learners have a role to play. For example, opportunities to foster professional learning may occur as a result of performance management arrangements. The performance review held between teacher and team leader may be described as 'an opportunity for the teacher and the team leader to reflect on the teacher's performance in a structured way, to recognise achievements and to discuss areas for improvement and professional development'. Rather like former appraisal interviews (see Gunter, 1996), the performance review could facilitate professional learning if it encourages:

- reflection and self-knowledge;
- data collection;
- target-setting to identify learning goals and pathways;
- learning to become integral with professional activity;
- development of a collective and conscious competence;
- professional discussion which encourages all three learning loops (see above).

But it could hinder professional learning if it:

- is superficial and fails to engender internalisation;
- is mistrusting due to personal or power relationships;
- is supported by inadequate resources;
- is oblivious of learning styles;
- is detrimental to learning relationships because feedback is judgemental and damaging;
- is only supportive of single-loop learning (see above);
- is mismatched to adult learning.

How may leaders use coaching, mentoring and networking mechanisms to enhance professional development and help to create professional learning communities within their own organisations?

The role of coaching and mentoring

To become learning organisations, organisations need to create the conditions in which adults will commit themselves to collective professional learning. Headteachers, college principals and team leaders may face significant challenges as they assume leadership of organisation-based professional growth and development. In the development of unique learning communities, professional development is needed for key staff, including the training of teachers as coaches and mentors. Given time for necessary professional collaboration, the availability of coaches and mentors can in turn facilitate the capacity of all teachers as learners. Parsloe and Wray (2000) offer the following definition of the overall aim of coaching and mentoring within the learning organisation:

> the aim is to help and support people to manage their own learning in order that they may maximise their potential, develop their skills, improve their performance and enable them to become the person they want to be.

Enabling learners to become the person they want to be is of importance with respect to retention, motivation and performance. The notion of the teacher's professional self has been explored via teachers' self-conception of themselves as teachers (see Keltchermans, 1993). In this work, five components were emphasised, all of which may be influential and important to the way in which a teacher perceives specific job situations, gives meaning to them and acts in them.

1	Self-image	(Who am I as a teacher?)
2	Self-esteem	(How good am I at doing my job as a teacher?)
3	Job motivation	(What motivates me in this job, what keeps me going or makes me decide to quit?)
4	Task perception	(What must I do to be a proper teacher?)
5	The future perspective	(How do I think about my future life as a teacher and how do I feel about it?)

Activity 9.5

Self-conception

Analyse your own self-conception of yourself as a teacher using the five headings provided by Keltchermans (1993).

In each case, how might individual, collective or organisational professional learning help or hinder the development of your self-conception?

The role of networking

Teachers often learn best from and with other teachers within a climate of trust and collaboration. This new challenge of collaboration and networking both internally and externally requires organisational structures which minimise teachers' isolation and foster dialogue and discussion. Teachers and leaders need to promote effective practice in internal networking and to stimulate a culture of discussion and reflection. They need to be active in seeking access to external networking to enhance professional learning, not least with other schools and colleges locally, regionally and nationally.

Benefits of networking may be summarised as:

- promotes a climate for the exchange of ideas;
- professionals can learn from each other across a variety of contexts;
- professionals can work together to achieve personal and organisational targets;
- teachers and associate staff can learn from each other to inform future practice;
- promotes opportunities for inter-organisation exchange locally, nationally and internationally;
- share, disseminate and celebrate effective practice;
- develop knowledge in practice and knowledge of practice (see Chapter 1).

To further develop knowledge in practice and knowledge of practice, teachers would benefit from becoming members of a learning community or an identified community of practice which facilitates reflection and values their professional learning. However, depending on the prevailing collaborative and professional development culture created by leaders within individual organisations, teachers may experience more or less difficulty in learning with and from other teachers. Given stakeholder and 'expert' input, such a community would have the potential to enable teachers to develop as reflective practitioners and foster the development of identities which encompass self-worth, satisfaction and retention.

Possible 'expert' partners include LEAs and HEIs. LEAs may provide a coordinating role in network development by identifying local needs, knowing 'interesting' practice, making links and verifying the quality of practice.

In the case of HEI partners, they may become a partner in the community and foster learning through the promotion of teacher research activities. Offering a note of caution, however, a study undertaken by Peters (2002) suggested that research partnership and collaboration with HEIs may be hampered by individual teachers' struggles in the face of non-supportive personal, structural and cultural conditions. This may be damaging to some teachers in terms of anxiety, guilt, self-doubt, intensification of workload, increased pressure on time, criticism from colleagues and missed opportunities for learning.

Activity 9.6

Partners in a learning community

Consider the development of a learning community within your own professional context.

- Who would be partners in this learning community and why?
- How might each of the partners benefit?
- What difficulties might need to be overcome?

The future

Although research to elucidate how organisations become effective learning communities is still underway, it is clear that a major role for leaders in the area of teacher professional development is to build leadership capacity within their organisations and among staff within their organisations to create, nurture and maintain a vital, self-renewing and authentic learning community. However, the inertia in leadership and management cultures in some organisations may be hard to break.

It is hoped that in the future, informed professional judgement on the part of all staff within schools and colleges will be supported by leadership, networking and collaboration. Professional learning with high leverage and therefore high impact on teaching and learning in classrooms is likely to encompass the following:

- the use of external expertise;
- observation and feedback;
- peer support;
- sustaining and embedding professional learning through coaching and mentoring;
- the development of professional learning communities;
- increased capacity for learning through the use of practice-based research.

Given an emphasis on teacher learning, leadership learning, organisation-to-organisation learning and network-to-network learning, how can emergent good practices be communicated to all staff in schools and colleges? Good practice does not travel well, and peer-networking, coaching and mentoring are needed to ensure that this transfer is made better. Are there more costs than benefits associated with coaching, mentoring and peer-networking? In using these mechanisms to realise the raising of achievement for young people in schools and colleges, it is suggested that there are potentially far more benefits than costs. It is hoped in the future that these mechanisms will become routine.

Extended activities

The remaining two extended activities in this chapter are intended to further engage and challenge the reader with issues central to successful coaching, mentoring and peer-networking. The first activity sets out to explore the possible individual and organisational benefits to emerge from the creation of a community of practice network. The second activity enables the reader to explore the possible role of teacher leadership in fostering the establishment of professional learning communities.

Extended activity 9.7

Enhancing professional development by exploring possible benefits to emerge from the creation of a community of practice network

Context

The following is an example of a CPD flyer produced by a university.

> *Creating a professional learning community in your organisation*
>
> Do you have a vision for your organisation, at the heart of a community, in which **all** participants are actively learning and developing? We can play a part in helping you achieve this.
>
> - A partnership with us can help you build your organisation's capacity for improvement.
> - We can support you in developing an improvement strategy that raises standards and also helps you in recruiting, retaining and developing all your staff.
> - Modules can be delivered in your organisation and in-house accreditation will be useful in marketing your organisation to learners and prospective staff.
> - We can support you in the creation of progression pathways that can potentially transform community involvement in learning. For example, community members becoming para-professionals and developing further to become teachers.
> - We can negotiate with you exactly what outcomes you want assessed and recognised. For example, some organisations have arranged to accredit their staff's involvement in producing and implementing the development plan.
> - We can help you address the long-standing challenge of how to ensure CPD really impacts practice.
> - You can give structure and rigour to your CPD by adopting the Master's degree pathway. This indicates how seriously you take staff development.
> - We can offer blended learning that emphasises organisation-focused activities. It need not disrupt the work of busy practitioners working in the most challenging situations.

> - We can offer trained coaches to enable the enhancement of specific skills and help embed new practices.
> - We can offer tutors to act as mentors in order to ensure ongoing professional learning and access to additional networks to help bring new practical insights as well as research insights into the organisation.

Aims

- To critically reflect upon personal and whole-organisation benefits which may arise from coaching opportunities in a community of practice network.
- To critically reflect upon personal and whole-organisation benefits which may arise from mentoring opportunities in a community of practice network.
- To critically reflect upon personal and whole-organisation benefits which may arise from other activities in a community of practice network.
- To review existing organisation professional development policy in the light of the above critical reflection.

Steps

This activity consists of four steps. Steps may be undertaken by individuals working alone or in a group.

- *Step 1* involves critical reflection on personal or whole-organisation benefits which could arise by coaching activities fostered externally (or internally) via a partner within a community of practice.
- *Step 2* involves critical reflection on personal or whole-organisation benefits which could arise by mentoring activities fostered externally (or internally) via a partner within a community of practice.
- *Step 3* involves critical reflection on personal or whole-organisation benefits which could arise by other activities fostered externally (or internally) via a partner within a community of practice.
- *Step 4* involves undertaking a review of current organisation professional development policy and suggestion of possible items of modification in the light of the above critical reflection.

Step 1

Write down ideas as they occur for possible personal and whole-organisation benefits to emerge from coaching either internally or externally.

Ideas for possible benefits include:

Benefit	Personal?	Whole organisation?	Internal coaching?	External coaching?	Justification for action?

continued

Step 2

Write down ideas as they occur for possible personal and whole-organisation benefits to emerge from mentoring either internally or externally.

Ideas for possible benefits include:

Benefit	Personal?	Whole organisation?	Internal mentoring?	External mentoring?	Justification for action?

Step 3

Write down ideas as they occur for possible personal and whole-organisation benefits to emerge from other community of practice activities either internally or externally.

Ideas for possible benefits:

Benefit	Personal?	Whole organisation?	Internal activity?	External activity?	Justification for action?

Step 4

Obtain a copy of the current organisation's professional development policy. In the light of the above critical reflection, make suggestions for possible improvements so that professional development may be enhanced for yourself and for others by the outcomes of your reflection. Consider making this available to the organisation's senior management team.

Extended activity 9.8

Teacher leadership and professional learning communities: developing human capital

Context

Although leadership in UK educational organisations has been traditionally associated with individuals such as headteachers and college principals, there is a growing discussion concerning the possible benefits of shared leadership, leadership teams and distributed leadership. In a recent article, Harris (2003) explores the concept of 'teacher leadership', which may be summarised as the empowerment of teachers to exercise leadership irrespective of their position within the organisation. Little (1995) suggests that where teachers learn from one another through mentoring, observation peer-coaching and mutual reflection, the possibilities of generating teacher leadership are significantly enhanced. The benefits of teacher leadership can include greater effectiveness, improved practices and improved collaboration. Harris (2003) suggests that where teacher leadership functions optimally it can contribute directly to the establishment of professional learning communities within and between organisations. Given the possible benefits of empowering teacher leaders and developing human capital in terms of decision-making, sense of purpose, collaboration and responsibility for outcomes, what structures within the organisation will enable this to occur? What opportunities can be developed to enable teacher leaders to build capacity for improvement and develop and share new practices?

Aims

- To establish current opportunities for teachers to work together and lead change and improvement.
- To reflect upon the pros and cons of encouraging and supporting teacher leadership within the organisation.
- To determine possible interventions using coaching, mentoring and peer-networking to promote teacher leadership and hence the possibility of the emergence of a professional learning community within the organisation.

Steps

This activity consists of three steps. Steps may be undertaken by individuals working alone or in a group.

- *Step 1* involves a critical audit to establish current opportunities for teachers to work together, engage in decision-making, and lead change and improvement within the organisation for which they have assumed ownership.
- *Step 2* involves a critical reflection on the pros and cons of encouraging and supporting teacher leadership within the organisation. Advantages and disadvantages should be explored using the notions of empowerment and of central leadership control.
- *Step 3* involves drawing upon the pros and cons of encouraging and supporting teacher leadership to create a list of descriptions of coaching, mentoring and peer-networking interventions to maximise advantages and minimise disadvantages. In introducing an intervention, consider how it will foster the development of a professional learning community within the organisation.

continued

Step 1

Undertake a critical audit to establish current opportunities for teachers to work together, engage in decision-making, and lead change and improvement within the organisation for which they have taken ownership.

Example of current opportunity (e.g. timetabling)	*Work together?*	*Decision-making?*	*Lead change?*	*Ownership?*

Are opportunities for teachers to work in this way prevalent within the organisation? How does this impact upon capacity building for improvement and the development of a professional learning community within the organisation?

Step 2

Undertake a critical reflection on the pros and cons of encouraging and supporting teacher leadership within the organisation.

Task or service (e.g. improve achievement)	*Advantages of teacher empowerment*	*Disadvantages of teacher empowerment*	*Advantages of central leadership control*	*Disadvantages of central leadership control*

Step 3

Drawing upon the advantages of teacher empowerment and the disadvantages of central control listed in Step 2 (above), create a list of descriptions of coaching, mentoring and peer-networking interventions to maximise advantages and minimise disadvantages. In introducing an intervention, consider how it will foster the development of a professional learning community within the organisation.

Task or service	*Nature of intervention*	*How will this foster the development of a professional learning community?*

References

Adelman, N.E. and Panton Walking-Eagle, K. (1997) Teachers, Time and School Reform, in A. Hargreaves (ed.) *ASCD Yearbook: Rethinking Educational Change with Heart and Mind*, Virginia: Association for Supervision and Curriculum Development.

Alexander, P. A. and Murphy, P.K. (1999) Nurturing the Seeds of Transfer: a domain-specific perspective, *International Journal of Educational Research*, 31, 561–576.

Atkins, S. and Murphy, K. (1993) Reflection: a review of the literature, *Journal of Advanced Nursing*, 18(1), 188–192.

Barker, P. (1998) 'Hard Road to Travel? Try a Coach', *Observer*, 12 July.

Beatty, B. (2000) Teachers Leading their Own Professional Growth: self-directed reflection and collaboration and changes in perception of self and work in secondary school teachers, *Journal of In-Service Education*, 26, 73–97.

Beaumont, P. B. (1994) *Human Resource Management: Key Concepts and Skills*, London: Sage Publications.

Beels, C. and Powell, D. (1994) *Mentoring with Newly Qualified Teachers: The Practical Guide*, Leeds: CCDU University of Leeds.

Bell, C. (2002) *Managers as Mentors*, San Francisco, CA: Berrett-Koehler.

Blackstone, Baroness (2000) Speech to the FEFC's AGM reported in the *AoC and DfEE Teaching Pay Initiative Guidance*, London: AoC.

Bleach, K. (1999) *The Induction and Mentoring of Newly Qualified Teachers: A New Deal for Teachers*, London: David Fulton.

Bleach, K. (2000) *The Newly Qualified Secondary Teacher's Handbook: Meeting the Standards in Secondary and Middle Schools*, London: David Fulton.

Bolam, R. (2000) Emerging Policy Trends: some implications for continuing professional development, *Journal of In-Service Education*, 26(2), 267–280.

Bowerman, J. and Collins, G. (1999) The Coaching Network: a program for individual and organisational development, *Journal of Educational Administration*, 33(5), 29–44.

Bredeson, P.V. (2000) Teacher Learning as Work and at Work: exploring the content and contexts of teacher professional development, *Journal of In-Service Education*, 26(1), 63–72.

Bredeson, P.V. and Johansson, O. (2000) The School Principal's Role in Teacher Professional Development, *Journal of In-Service Education*, 26(2), 385–401.

Brookfield, S.D. (1986) *Understanding and Facilitating Adult Learning*, San Francisco, CA: Jossey-Bass.

Brown, K. (2001) Mentoring and the Retention of Newly Qualified Language Teachers, *Cambridge Journal of Education*, 31(1), 89–102.

Bubb, S. (2000) *The Effective Induction of Newly Qualified Primary Teachers: An Induction Tutor's Handbook*, London: David Fulton.

Bubb, S. (2001) *A Newly Qualified Teacher's Manual*, London: David Fulton.

Burchell, H., Dyson, J. and Rees, M. (2002) Making a Difference: a study of the impact of continuing professional development on professional practice, *Journal of In-Service Education*, 28(2), 219–229.

Butcher, J. (2002) A Case for Mentor Challenge? The problem of learning to teach post-16, *Mentoring and Tutoring*, 10(3), 197–220.

Butler, T. and Chao, T. (2001) Partners for Change: students as effective technology mentors, *Active Learning in Higher Education*, 2(2), 101–113.

Cartwright, J., Andrews, T. and Webley, P. (1999) A Methodology for Cultural Measurement and Change: a case study, *Total Quality Management*, 10, 121–128.

Clement, M. and Vandenberghe, R. (2001) How School Leaders can Promote Teachers' Professional Development: an account from the field, *School Leadership and Management*, 21(1), 43–57.

Clutterbuck, D. (1991) *Everyone Needs a Mentor*, London: Institute of Personnel and Development.

Clutterbuck, D. and Megginson, D. (1999) *Mentoring Executives and Directors*, London: Butterworth.

Cochran-Smith, M. and Lytle, S. (1999) Teacher Learning in Communities, *Review of Research in Education*, 24, 249–306.

Collarbone, P. (2000) Aspirant Heads, *Managing Schools Today*, June/July, 28–32.

Daloz, L. (ed.) (1998) Mentorship, in M.W. Galbraith *Adult Learning Methods: A Guide to Effective Instruction*, Florida: Krieger.

Davies, R. and Preston, M. (2002) An Evaluation of the Impact of Continuing Professional Development on Personal and Professional Lives, *Journal of In-Service Education*, 28(2), 231–254.

Day, C. (1999) *Developing Teachers: The Challenge of Lifelong Learning*, London: Falmer Press.

Day, C. and Harris, A. (2003) Teacher Leadership, Reflective Practice and School Improvement, in *International Handbook of Educational Administration*, pp. 724–749, Dordrecht: Kluwer Academic.

Day, C., Harris, A. and Hadfield, M. (2001) Grounding Knowledge of Schools in Stakeholder Realities: a multi-perspective study of effective school leaders, *School Leadership and Management*, 21(1), 19–42.

Day, C., Hadfield, M. and Kellow, M. (2002) Schools as Learning Communities: Building Capacity Through Network Learning, *Education 3–13*, October, 19–22.

Dean, P. (2001) Blood on the Tracks: an accusation and proposal, *Journal of In-Service Education*, 27, 491–499.

DfEE (1999) *The Induction Period for Newly Qualified Teachers*, Circular 5/99, London: DfEE.

DfEE (2000a) *Performance Management in Schools: Performance Management Framework*, London: Stationery Office.

DfEE (2000b) *Performance Management in Schools: Model Performance Management Policy*, London: Stationery Office.

DfEE (2001a) *The Teacher Pay Initiative*, London: DfEE.

DfEE (2001b) *Schools: Building on Success*, London: Stationery Office.

DfES (2001a) *Learning and Teaching: A Strategy for Professional Development*, London: Stationery Office.

DfES (2001b) *Good Value CPD: A Code of Practice for Providers of Professional Development for Teachers*, London: Stationery Office.

DfES (2001c) *Teachers' Standards Framework: Helping you Develop*, London: Stationery Office.

DfES (2001d) *Schools Achieving Success*, London: Stationery Office.

DfES (2001e) *Investors in People and Continuing Professional Development*, Sudbury: DfES Publications.

DfES (2001f) *Helping You Develop: Guidance on Producing a Professional Development Record*, Nottingham: DfES Publications.

DfES (2002) *Success for All*, London: Department for Education and Skills.

DfES (2003) *The Core Principles: Teaching and Learning, School Improvement, System Wide Reform*, Consultation Text, CSAG 03/03, London: Department for Education and Skills.

Dignard, K. (2002) *Mentoring Handbook – Department of Family Medicine*, Ottawa: University of Ottawa.

Down, B., Hogan, C. and Chadbourne, R. (1999) Making Sense of Performance Management: official rhetoric and teachers' reality, *Asia-Pacific Journal of Teacher Education*, 27, 11–24.

Downey, M. (2001) *Effective Coaching*, London: Texere.

Dufour, R. and Berkey, T. (1995) The Principal as Staff Developer, *Journal of Staff Development*, 16(4), 2–6.

Earley, P. and Kinder, K. (1994) *Initiation Rights: Effective Induction Practices for New Teachers*, Windsor: NFER.

Earley, P., Evans, J., Collarbone, P., Gold, A. and Halpin, D. (2002) *Establishing the Current State of School Leadership in England*, http://www.dfes.gov.uk/research/data/uploadfiles/RR336.pdf.

Elmore, R.F. (2000) *Building a New Structure for School Leadership*, Washington, DC: Albert Shanker Institute.

Eraut, M. (1994) *Developing Professional Knowledge and Competence*, London: Falmer Press.

Evans, L. (2001) Delving Deeper into Morale, Job Satisfaction and Motivation among Education Professionals: re-examining the leadership dimension, *Educational Management and Administration*, 29, 291–306.

Ewans, D. (2001) *Observation of Teaching and Learning in Adult Education*, London: LSDA.

Fabian, H. and Simpson, A. (2002) Mentoring the Experienced Teacher, *Mentoring and Tutoring*, 10(2), 117–125.

FEDA (1995) *Learning Styles*, London: FEDA.

FEFC (1999) *Standards Fund*, Coventry: FEFC.

FEFC (2000) *Circular 00/15*, Coventry: FEFC.

FENTO (2000) *Standards for Teaching and Supporting Learning in Further Education in England and Wales*, London: FENTO.

FENTO (2001) *Standards for Teaching and Supporting Learning in Further Education in England and Wales*, London: FENTO.

Fidler, B. and Atton, T. (1999) *Poorly Performing Staff in Schools and How to Manage Them*, London: Routledge.

Flecknoe, M. (2000) Can Continuing Professional Development for Teachers be Shown to Raise Pupils' Achievement?, *Journal of In-Service Education*, 26(3), 437–457.

Fleming, P. (2000) *The Art of Middle Management in Secondary Schools: A Guide to Effective Subject and Team Leadership*, London: David Fulton.

Friedman, A. and Phillips, M. (2001) Leaping the CPD Hurdle: a study of the barriers and drivers to participation in continuing professional development, http://www.leeds.ac.uk/educol/documents/00001892.htm.

Fullan, M. (2001) *Leading in a Culture of Change*, San Francisco, CA: Jossey-Bass.

Galbraith, M.W. and Cohen, H.H. (eds) (1995) *Mentoring: New Strategies and Challenges*, San Francisco, CA: Jossey-Bass.

Gardiner, C. (1998) Mentoring: Towards a Professional Friendship, *Mentoring and Tutoring*, 6, 77–84.

Garratt, B. (1987) *The Learning Organisation*, Aldershot: Gower.

Garvey, B. and Alred, G. (2000) Educating Mentors, *Mentoring and Tutoring*, 8(2), 113–126.

Gibb, S. (1994) Evaluating Mentoring, *Education and Training*, 36(5), 32–39.

Gleeson, D. and Husbands, C. (eds) (2001) *The Performing School: Managing, Teaching and Learning in a Performance Culture*, London: RoutledgeFalmer.

Gronn, P. (2000) Distributed Properties: A New Architecture for Leadership, *Educational Management and Administration*, 28(3), 317–338.

GTC (2002) *Teachers on Teaching: A Survey of the Teaching Profession*, http://www.educationguardian.co.uk.

Gunter, H. (1996) Appraisal and the School as a Learning Organisation, *School Organisation*, 16(1), 89–100.

Gunter, H. and Ribbins, P. (2003) The Field of Educational Leadership: studying maps and mapping studies, *British Journal of Educational Studies*, 51(3), 254–281.

Guskey, T.R. (1995) Results-oriented Professional Development: in search of an optimal mix of effective practices, http://www.ncrel.org/sdrs/areas/rpl_esys/pdlitrev.htr.

Hansford, B., Tennent, L. and Ehrich, L.C. (2002) Business Mentoring: help or hindrance?, *Mentoring and Tutoring*, 10(2), 101–115.

Harris, A. (2000) What Works in School Improvement? Lessons from the field and future directions, *Educational Research*, 42(1), 1–11.

Harris, A. (2001) Building the Capacity for School Improvement, *School Leadership and Management*, 21(3), 261–270.

Harris, A. (2002) Effective Leadership in Schools Facing Challenging Contexts, *School Leadership and Management*, 22(1), 15–27.

Harris, A. (2003) Teacher Leadership as Distributed Leadership: heresy, fantasy or possibility?, *School Leadership and Management*, 23(3), 313–324.

Harris, A. and Chapman, C. (2002) *Democratic Leadership for School Improvement in Challenging Contexts*, Paper Presented at the International Congress on School Effectiveness and Improvement, Copenhagen.

Harris, A. and Hopkins, D. (1999) Teaching and Learning and the Challenge of Educational Reform, *School Effectiveness and School Improvement*, 10, 257–267.

Harris, A. and Lambert, L. (2003a) *Building Capacity for School Improvement*, Maidenhead: Open University Press.

Harris, A. and Lambert, L. (2003b) *What is Leadership Capacity?*, Nottingham: National College for School Leadership.

Harris, A., Busher, H. and Wise, C. (2001) Effective Training for Subject Leaders, *Journal of In-Service Education*, 27(1), 83–94.

Harrison, R. (2001) A Strategy for Professional Development, *Professional Development Today*, summer, 9–20.

Hayes, D. (1999) Mentors' Expectations of Student Primary Teachers, *Mentoring and Tutoring*, 7(1), 67–78.

Hayes, D. (2000) *The Handbook for Newly Qualified Teachers: Meeting the Standards in Primary and Middle Schools*, London: David Fulton.

Hay McBer (2000) The Lessons of Leadership, http://www.transforminglearning.co.uk.

Higgins, S. and Leat, D. (1997) Horses for Courses: what is effective teacher development?, *British Journal of In-Service Education*, 23(3), 303–314.

Higgins-D'Alessandro, A. and Sadh, D. (1997) The Dimensions and Measurement of School Culture: understanding school culture as the basis for school reform, *International Journal of Educational Research*, 27, 553–569.

Honey, P. and Mumford, A. (1992) *Manual of Learning Styles*, Maidenhead: P. Honey.

Hopkins, D. and Jackson, D. (2002) Building the Capacity for Leading and Learning, in A. Harris *et al. Effective Leadership for School Improvement*, London: RoutledgeFalmer.

Hopper, B. (2001) The Role of the HEI Tutor in Initial Teacher Education School-based Placements, *Mentoring and Tutoring*, 9(3), 211–222.

Hughes, C. (1999) Foreword, in P. Martinez *Learning from Continuous Professional Development*, London: FEDA.

Imel, S. (1992) *Reflective Practice in Adult Education*, Columbus, OH: ERIC Clearinghouse on Adult, Career and Vocational Education.

Imel, S. (1998) *Using Adult Learning Principles in Adult Basic Literacy Education*, Columbus, OH: ERIC Clearinghouse on Adult, Career and Vocational Education.

Jackson, D. (2000) The School Improvement Journey: perspectives on leadership, *School Leadership and Management*, 20(1), 61–78.

Jackson, D. and Payne, G. (2002) *The Headteacher – Guardian of Leverage for School Improvement*, Nottingham: National College for School Leadership.

Jossi, F. (1997) Mentoring in Changing Times, *Training*, 34, 50–53.

Joyce, B. and Showers, B. (1988) *Student Achievement Through Staff Development*, New York: Longman.

Katzenmeyer, M. and Moller, G. (2001) *Awakening the Sleeping Giant: Helping Teachers Develop as Leaders*, Thousand Oaks, CA: Corwin.

Kearsley, G. and Shneiderman, B. (1998) Engagement Theory: A Framework for Technology-based Teaching and Learning, *Educational Technology*, September/October, 20–23.

Keltchermans, G. (1993) Getting the Story and Understanding the Lives: from career stories to professional development, *Teaching and Teacher Education*, 9(5/6), 443–456.

Kerka, S. (1997) *New Perspectives on Mentoring*, ERIC Digests No 194, Columbus, OH: ERIC Clearinghouse on Adult, Career and Vocational Education.

Kibby, L. (2003) The Mentoring Millennium – the corporate tool for 2021, http://www.mentoring.org/common/effective-mentoring-practices.

Kilburg, R.R. (1996) Towards a Conceptual Understanding and Definition of Executive Coaching, *Consulting Psychology Journal: Practice and Research*, 48(2), 134–144.

Kinder, K., Harland, J. and Wootten, M. (1991) *The Impact of School Focused INSET on Classroom Practice*, Slough: NFER.

Klasen, N. and Clutterbuck, D. (2002) *Implementing Mentoring Schemes*, Oxford: Butterworth-Heinemann.

Knowles, M.S. (1980) *The Modern Practice of Adult Education: From Pedagogy to Andragogy*, River Grove, USA: Follett.

Kolb, D. (1985) *Learning Style Inventory: Technical Manual*, Boston, MA: Hay McBer.

Kullman, J. (1998) Mentoring and the Development of Reflective Practice: concepts and context, *System*, 26, 471–484.

Kydd, L., Crawford, M. and Riches, C. (eds) (1997) *Professional Development for Educational Management*, Buckingham: Open University Press.

Lacey, K. (1999) *Making Mentoring Happen*, New South Wales: Business and Professional Publishing.

Landsberg, M. (1996) *The Tao of Coaching*, London: Harper Collins.

Law, S. (1999) Leadership for Learning: the changing culture of professional development in schools, *Journal of Educational Administration*, 37, 66–79.

Law, S. and Glover, D. (1996) *Towards Coherence in the Management of Professional Development Planning*, Cambridge: BEMAS Research Conference.

Learning and Skills Council (LSC) (2003) *Development Plans*, Circular 03/09, Coventry: LSC.

Lewis, G. (2000) *The Mentoring Manager*, London: Pearson.

Lieberman, A. and Miller, L. (2000) Teaching and Teacher Development: a new synthesis for a new century, in R. S. Brandt (ed.) *Education in a New Era*, Virginia: ASCD.

Little, J.W. (1995) Contested Ground: the basis of teacher leadership in two restructuring high schools, *The Elementary School Journal*, 96(1), 47–63.

Locatelli, V. and West, M. (1996) On Elephants and Blind Researchers: methods for accessing culture in organisations, *Leadership and Organization Development Journal*, 17, 12–21.

Lumby, J. (2003) Distributed Leadership in Colleges: leading or misleading?, *Educational Management and Administration*, 31(3), 283–292.

MacBeath, J. (2001) Ofsted as a Learning Organisation – hope for the future, *Education Review*, 14(2), 9–12.

McCann, I. and Radford, R. (1993) Mentoring for Teachers: the collaborative approach, in B.J. Caldwell and E.M. Carter (eds) *The Return of the Mentor: Strategies for Workplace Learning*, Washington, DC: Falmer Press.

Malderez, A. and Bodoczky, C. (1996) *Mentor Courses*, Cambridge: Cambridge University Press.

Martinez, P. (1999) *Learning from Continuous Professional Development*, London: FEDA.

Maynard, T. (2000) Learning to Teach or Learning to Manage Mentors? Experiences of school-based teacher training, *Mentoring and Tutoring*, 8(1), 17–30.

Montgomery, D. (1999) *Teacher Appraisal Through Classroom Observation*, London: David Fulton.

Moon, B. (2000) A Debate we Can't Dodge, *Times Educational Supplement*, March, 17.

Moon, J.A. (2002) *Reflection in Learning and Professional Development*, London: Kogan Page.

Moonen, B. and Voogt, J. (1998) Using Networks to Support the Professional Development of Teachers, *Journal of In-Service Education*, 24(1), 99–110.

Muijs, D. and Harris, A. (2003) Teacher Leadership: improvement through empowerment?, *Educational Management and Administration*, 31(4), 437–448.

Mumford, A. (1995) Learning Styles and Mentoring, *Industrial and Commercial Training*, 27(8), 4–7.

NCSL (2002) *Why Networked Learning Communities?*, Nottingham: National College for School Leadership.

O'Brien, J. and MacBeath, J. (1999) Co-ordinating Staff Development: the training and development of staff development co-ordinators, *Journal of In-Service Education*, 25, 69–83.

Ofsted (2002) Leadership and Management Training for Headteachers, Report by HMI, http://www.ofsted.gov.uk.

Ofsted (2003) *Teachers' Early Professional Development* (HMI 1394), http://www.ofsted.gov.uk.

Ofsted/ALI (2001) *The Common Inspection Framework*, London: ALI and Ofsted.

Oldroyd, D. and Hall, V. (1988) *Managing Professional Development and INSET: A Handbook for Schools and Colleges*, Bristol: NDCSMT, Bristol University School of Education.

O'Sullivan, F. (1997) Learning Organisations: reengineering schools for life-long learning, *School Leadership and Management*, 17(2), 217–230.

Parsloe, E. (1992) *Coaching, Mentoring and Assessing*, London: Kogan Page.

Parsloe, E. and Wray, M. (2000) *Coaching and Mentoring*, London: Kogan Page.

Pedler, M., Boydell, T. and Burgoyne, J. (1988) *Learning Company Project: A Report on Work Undertaken October 1987 to April 1988*, Sheffield: The Training Agency.

Peeke, G. (2002) *Issues in Continuing Professional Development*, London: LSDA.

Pegg, M. (1999) The Art of Mentoring, *Industrial and Commercial Training*, 31(4), 27–38.

Peters, J. (1991) Strategies for Reflective Practice, in R. Brockett (ed.) *Professional Development for Educators of Adults*, New Directions for Adult and Continuing Education, 51, San Francisco, CA: Jossey-Bass.

Peters, J. (2002) *Expecting Too Much From School/University Partnerships for School Improvement*, Paper Presented at the British Educational Research Association, University of Exeter, 12–14 September, http://www.leeds.ac.uk/educol/documents/00002132.htm.

Phillips, R. (1995) Coaching for Higher Performance, *Executive Development*, 8(7), 5–7.

Ponzio, R.C. (1987) The Effects of Having a Partner when Teachers Study Their own Teaching, *Teacher Education Quarterly*, 14(3), 25–40.

Portner, H. (2001) *Training Mentors is Not Enough*, California, CA: Corwin Press.

Power, M. (1997) *The Audit Society*, Oxford: Oxford University Press.

Ragins, B.R. and Cotton, J.L. (1999) Mentor Functions and Outcomes: a comparison of men and women in formal and informal mentoring relationships, *Journal of Applied Psychology*, 84(4), 529–550.

Redshaw, B. (2000) Do We Really Understand Coaching? How can we make it better? *Industrial and Commercial Training*, 32(3), 106–108.

Rhodes, C.P. (2001) *Resource Management for Schools: A Handbook for Staff Development Activities*, London: David Fulton.

Rhodes, C.P. and Beneicke, S. (2002) Coaching, Mentoring and Peer-networking: challenges for the management of teacher professional development in schools, *Journal of In-Service Education*, 28(2), 297–309.

Rhodes, C.P. and Beneicke, S. (2003) Professional Development Support for Poorly Performing Teachers: challenges and opportunities for school managers in addressing teacher learning needs, *Journal of In-Service Education*, 29(1), 123–140.

Rhodes, C.P. and Houghton-Hill, S. (2000) The Linkage of Continuing Professional Development and the Classroom Experience of Pupils: barriers perceived by senior managers in some secondary schools, *Journal of In-Service Education*, 26(3), 423–435.

Rhodes, C. P., Nevill, A. and Allan, J. L. (in press) Valuing and Supporting Teachers: a survey of teacher satisfaction, dissatisfaction, morale and retention within an English local education authority (Research in Education).

Rider, L. (2002) Coaching As a Strategic Intervention, *Industrial and Commercial Training*, 34(6), 233–236.

Robbins, P. (1995) Peer Coaching: quality through collaborative work, in J. Block, S.F. Everson and T.R. Guskey (eds) *School Improvement Programs: A Handbook for Educational Leaders*, New York: Scholastic Press.

Rogers, A. (1996) *Teaching Adults*, Buckingham: Open University Press.

Ross, J.A. and Regan, E.M. (1993) Sharing Professional Experience: its impact on professional development, *Teaching and Teacher Education*, 9(1), 91–106.

Rowe, K.J. and Sykes, J. (1989) The Impact of Professional Development on Teachers' Self-Perceptions, *Teaching and Teacher Education*, 5, 129–141.

Sachs, J. (2001) Teacher Professional Identity: competing discourses, competing outcomes, *Journal of Education Policy*, 16(2), 149–161.

Scandura, T.A., Tejada, M.J., Werther, W.B. and Lankau, M.J. (1996) Perspectives upon Mentoring, *Leadership and Organisation Development Journal*, 17(3), 50–56.

Senge, P. (1992) *The Fifth Discipline: The Art and Practice of the Learning Organisation*, London: Doubleday.

Sergiovanni, T.J. (1999) Refocusing Leadership to Build Community, *The High School Magazine*, September, 12–15.

Shalaway, L. (1985) Peer Coaching . . . Does it Work? *Washington National Institute of Education Research and Development Notes*, September, 6–7.

Shea, G.F. (2002) *Mentoring*, California: Crisp Learning.

Silcock, P. (2002) Can We Manage Teacher Performance?, *Education 3–13*, October, 23–27.

Simons, P.R.J. (1999) Transfer of Learning: paradoxes for learners, *International Journal of Educational Research*, 31, 577–589.

Skiffington, S. and Zeus, P. (2000) *The Complete Guide to Coaching at Work*, London: McGraw Hill.

Smith, M. E. (2000) The Role of the Tutor in Initial Teacher Education, *Mentoring and Tutoring*, 8(2), 137–144.

Smith, P. V. (1999) Managing Continuing Professional Development to Support School-based Target Setting, *Journal of In-Service Education*, 25, 85–95.

Southworth, G. (2002) Instructional Leadership in Schools: reflections and empirical evidence, *School Leadership and Management*, 22(1), 73–91.

Sugrue, C. (2002) Irish Teachers' Experiences of Professional Learning: implications for policy and practice, *Journal of In-Service Education*, 28(2), 311–338.

Swafford, J. (1998) Teachers Supporting Teachers Through Peer Coaching, *Support for Learning*, 13(2), 54–58.

Swafford, J., Maltsberger, A., Button, K. and Furgerson, P. (1997) Peer Coaching for Facilitating Effective Literacy Instruction, in C.K. Kinzer, K.A. Hinchman and D.J. Leu (eds) *Inquiries in Literacy Theory and Practice*, Chicago, IL: National Reading Conference.

Swieringa, J. and Wierdsma, A. (1992) *Becoming a Learning Organisation: Beyond the Learning Curve*, Wokingham: Addison Wesley.

Tharp, R.G. and Gallimore, R. (1988) *Rousing Minds to Life: Teaching, Learning and Schooling in Social Context*, Cambridge: Cambridge University Press.

Thompson, M. (2001) Towards Professional Learning Communities? in D. Gleeson and C. Husbands (eds) *The Performing School: Teaching and Learning in a Performance Culture*, London: RoutledgeFalmer.

Thornton, M., Bricheno, P. and Reid, I. (2002) Students' Reasons for Wanting to Teach in Primary School, *Research in Education*, 67, 33–43.

Torrance, E.P. (1984) *Mentor Relationships: How they Aid Creative Achievement, Endure, Change and Die*, New York: Bearly.

TTA (1999) *Supporting Induction Part 2: Support and Monitoring of Newly Qualified Teachers*, London: Teacher Training Agency.

TTA (2001) *The Role of the Induction Tutor: Principles and Guidance*, London: Teacher Training Agency.

Veenman, S. (1995) The Training of Coaching Skills: an implementation study, *Educational Studies*, 21, 415–431.

Veenman, S., De Laat, H. and Staring, C. (1998a) Evaluation of a Coaching Programme for Mentors of Beginning Teachers, *Journal of In-Service Education*, 24, 441–427.

Veenman, S., Visser, Y. and Wijkamp, N. (1998b) Implementation Effects of a Program for the Training of Coaching Skills with School Principals, *School Effectiveness and School Improvement*, 9, 135–156.

Walker, A. and Stott, K. (2000) Performance Improvement in Schools: a case of overdose?, *Educational Management and Administration*, 28, 63–76.

Wallace, M. (1996) When is Experiential Learning not Learning?, in G. Claxton, T. Atkinson, M. Osborn and M. Wallace (eds) *Liberating the Learner*, London: Routledge.

Watkins, C. and Whalley, C. (2000) Extending Feedback Forward, *Professional Development Today*, autumn.

Waugh, J.L. (2002) *Faculty Mentoring Guide – VCU School of Medicine*, Virginia: Virginia Commonwealth University.

Wendell, L.W. (1997) New Rule for Mentors and Mentees, *Philadelphia Business Journal*, 6 October, 2.

West-Burnham, J. and O'Sullivan, F. (1998) *Leadership and Professional Development in Schools; How to Promote Techniques for Effective Professional Learning*, London: Financial Times.

Whitmore, J. (1995) *Coaching for Performance: A Practical Guide to Growing Your Own Skills*, London: Nicholas Brealey.

Wikeley, F. (1998) Dissemination of Research as a Tool for School Improvement?, *School Leadership and Management*, 18, 59–73.

Williams, A., Prestage, S. and Bedward, J. (2001) Individualism to Collaboration: the significance of teacher culture to the induction of newly qualified teachers, *Journal of Education for Teaching*, 27(3), 253–267.

Wragg, C. (2000) Failing Teachers?, *Managing Schools Today*, February, 36–38.

Zachary, L.J. (2002) *The Role of Teacher as Mentor* (New Directions for Adult and Continuing Education, 93), San Francisco, CA: Jossey-Bass.

Index